death
and dying

Opposing Viewpoints ®

Other Books of Related Interest in the Opposing Viewpoints Series:

Additional Books in the Opposing Viewpoints Series:

death
Opposing Viewpoints ®
and dying

David L. Bender & Bruno Leone, *Series Editors*

Janelle Rohr, *Book Editor*

Neal Bernards & Bonnie Szumski, *Assistant Editors*

OPPOSING VIEWPOINTS SERIES ®

Greenhaven Press   577 Shoreview Park Road   St. Paul, Minnesota 55126

Library of Congress Cataloging-in-Publication Data

Death and dying.

(Opposing viewpoints series)
Bibliography: p.
Includes index.
1. Death—Psychological aspects.   2. Suicide—
Prevention.   3. Euthanasia—Moral and ethical aspects.
4. Terminal care.   I. Rohr, Janelle, 1963-
II. Title.   III. Series.
BF789.D4D345   1987   306.9   86-31943
ISBN 0-89908-393-5 (lib. bdg.)
ISBN 0-89908-368-4 (pbk.)

"Congress shall make no law...
abridging the freedom of speech,
or of the press."

First Amendment to the US Constitution

The basic foundation of our democracy is the first amendment
guarantee of freedom of expression. The *Opposing Viewpoints Series*
is dedicated to the concept of this basic freedom and the idea that
it is more important to practice it than to enshrine it.

Contents

Chapter 3: Is Infant Euthanasia Ever Justified?

Chapter 4: Should Euthanasia Be Allowed?

Chapter 5: Do the Dying Need Alternative Care?

Why Consider Opposing Viewpoints?

The Importance of Examining Opposing Viewpoints

The purpose of the Opposing Viewpoints Series, and this book in particular, is to present balanced, and often difficult to find, opposing points of view on complex and sensitive issues.

Probably the best way to become informed is to analyze the positions of those who are regarded as experts and well studied on issues. It is important to consider every variety of opinion in an attempt to determine the truth. Opinions from the mainstream of society should be examined. But also important are opinions that are considered radical, reactionary, or minority as well as those stigmatized by some other uncomplimentary label. An important lesson of history is the eventual acceptance of many unpopular and even despised opinions. The ideas of Socrates, Jesus, and Galileo are good examples of this.

Readers will approach this book with their own opinions on the issues debated within it. However, to have a good grasp of one's own viewpoint, it is necessary to understand the arguments of those with whom one disagrees. It can be said that those who do not completely understand their adversary's point of view do not fully understand their own.

A persuasive case for considering opposing viewpoints has been presented by John Stuart Mill in his work *On Liberty*. When examining controversial issues it may be helpful to reflect on this suggestion:

> The only way in which a human being can make some approach to knowing the whole of a subject, is by hearing what can be said about it by persons of every variety of opinion, and studying all modes in which it can be looked at by every character of mind. No wise man ever acquired his wisdom in any mode but this.

Analyzing Sources of Information

The Opposing Viewpoints Series includes diverse materials taken from magazines, journals, books, and newspapers, as well as statements and position papers from a wide range of individuals, organizations and governments. This broad spectrum of sources helps to develop patterns of thinking which are open to the consideration of a variety of opinions.

Pitfalls To Avoid

A pitfall to avoid in considering opposing points of view is that of regarding one's own opinion as being common sense and the most rational stance and the point of view of others as being only opinion and naturally wrong. It may be that another's opinion is correct and one's own is in error.

Another pitfall to avoid is that of closing one's mind to the opinions of those with whom one disagrees. The best way to approach a dialogue is to make one's primary purpose that of understanding the mind and arguments of the other person and not that of enlightening him or her with one's own solutions. More can be learned by listening than speaking.

It is my hope that after reading this book the reader will have a deeper understanding of the issues debated and will appreciate the complexity of even seemingly simple issues on which good and honest people disagree. This awareness is particularly important in a democratic society such as ours where people enter into public debate to determine the common good. Those with whom one disagrees should not necessarily be regarded as enemies, but perhaps simply as people who suggest different paths to a common goal.

Developing Basic Reading and Thinking Skills

In this book, carefully edited opposing viewpoints are purposely placed back to back to create a running debate; each viewpoint is preceded by a short quotation that best expresses the author's main argument. This format instantly plunges the reader into the midst of a controversial issue and greatly aids that reader in mastering the basic skill of recognizing an author's point of view.

A number of basic skills for critical thinking are practiced in the activities that appear throughout the books in the series. Some of the skills are:

Evaluating Sources of Information   The ability to choose from among alternative sources the most reliable and accurate source in relation to a given subject.

Separating Fact from Opinion   The ability to make the basic distinction between factual statements (those that can be demonstrated or verified empirically) and statements of opinion (those that are beliefs or attitudes that cannot be proved).

Identifying Stereotypes   The ability to identify oversimplified, exaggerated descriptions (favorable or unfavorable) about people and insulting statements about racial, religious or national groups, based upon misinformation or lack of information.

Recognizing Ethnocentrism   The ability to recognize attitudes or opinions that express the view that one's own race, culture, or group is inherently superior, or those attitudes that judge another culture or group in terms of one's own.

It is important to consider opposing viewpoints and equally important to be able to critically analyze those viewpoints. The activities in this book are designed to help the reader master these thinking skills. Statements are taken from the book's viewpoints and the reader is asked to analyze them. This technique aids the reader in developing skills that not only can be applied to the viewpoints in this book, but also to situations where opinionated spokespersons comment on controversial issues. Although the activities are helpful to the solitary reader, they are most useful when the reader can benefit from the interaction of group discussion.

Using this book and others in the series should help readers develop basic reading and thinking skills. These skills should improve the reader's ability to understand what they read. Readers should be better able to separate fact from opinion, substance from rhetoric and become better consumers of information in our media-centered culture.

This volume of the Opposing Viewpoints Series does not advocate a particular point of view. Quite the contrary! The very nature of the book leaves it to the reader to formulate the opinions he or she finds most suitable. My purpose as publisher is to see that this is made possible by offering a wide range of viewpoints which are fairly presented.

David L. Bender
Publisher

Introduction

"In a sense quite new to our culture, we have become ashamed of death, and we try to hide it, or hide ourselves away from it. It is, to our way of thinking, failure."

Dr. Lewis Thomas, *The Annals of the American Academy of Political and Social Sciences*, January 1980.

The ten-year coma of Karen Ann Quinlan presented a frightening possibility many people had never imagined—that one could be kept alive by science's life-saving machines long after the chance for a meaningful life had disappeared. Quinlan's case dramatized the benefits and pitfalls of the medical technology which prolonged her life.

In some ways, Quinlan represents a technological success. Less than fifty years ago there would have been no chance of saving the life of the 21-year-old New Jersey woman who slipped into a coma after consuming a mixture of drugs and alcohol. In March 1976, a year after the coma began, her parents won a landmark court battle allowing them to have her respirator disconnected. After the respirator was disconnected, Quinlan stayed alive for nine more years, until June 11, 1985. Her life during that period suggests technology's dark side. Huddled in a fetal position with feeding tubes connected to her body, Quinlan's world became an 8-by-10-foot room in a nursing home. She shrunk to sixty pounds and suffered recurring lung infections. It seemed highly unlikely that she would ever recover and lead a normal life. To many people, Karen Ann Quinlan's case became a metaphor for the worst of all possible worlds. It was argued that such deaths were unnatural and undignified because technology was used to prolong the dying process, not to save Quinlan's life.

Yet without technology, Quinlan's parents would not have had the choice they had. Their daughter simply would have died. The respirator gave her lungs the chance to recover so that by the time it was disconnected, Quinlan could breathe on her own. Those who opposed the parents' decision to disconnect their daughter's respirator pointed to cases of people waking from comas as evidence that Quinlan's situation might not have been hopeless after all. Furthermore, medical advances have had many obvious benefits which cannot be denied. For example, the low infant mortality rate in North America and Western Europe is a phenomenon unique to the late twentieth century. Until the last twenty-five years, it was not uncommon for a family to lose a child at birth or to a childhood illness. Sociologist Robert Fulton reports that at the turn of the century, one-half of all deaths in the United States were those of children under 15 years of age. Children today represent only five percent of all deaths, according to Fulton, the director of the University of Minnesota's Center for Death Education. Without modern medicine, many people now alive probably would have died in childhood, perhaps even Quinlan herself. Ironically, now that medicine has given people longer, healthier lives, the question of limiting technology has arisen.

Karen Ann Quinlan's case also focused attention on social attitudes toward death. Her lengthy stay in a nursing home dramatized how much the dying process has changed in the last hundred years. As dying has changed, so have related social values. Families today tend to be less intimately involved in caring for the dying on a day-to-day basis than they were 100 years ago. Eighty percent of the time, death now occurs in a hospital or nursing home with the dying person under the care of doctors and nurses. The primary job of these professionals is to fight death. Thus death seems to be a "failure" and not merely the course of nature, as it was perceived to be in the past. These attitudes have given rise to new terms that are now common to debates on death, terms like "heroic measures" and "right to die." In the past, there were no heroic measures to try and the right to die was rarely an issue because medicine was not capable of keeping dying people alive.

Just as the complex issues raised in the Quinlan case shaped the modern debate on death, so those issues provide the basis for the debates in *Death and Dying: Opposing Viewpoints*. The questions include: How Should One Cope with Death? How Can Suicide Be Prevented? Is Infant Euthanasia Ever Justified? Should Euthanasia Be Allowed? and Do the Dying Need Alternative Care? This book replaces two previous Greenhaven titles, *Death & Dying* (1980) and *Problems of Death* (1981). *Death and Dying* allows readers to explore the controversy modern medicine has raised—a controversy which faces more and more people as technology continues to change death.

How Should One Cope with Death?

death
and dying

1

VIEWPOINT

---

*"It is apparent that the process of
uncomplicated grief follows a relatively
predictable pattern."*

Grief Follows a
Predictable Pattern

J. Trig Brown and G. Alan Stoudemire

Several theories describe the process of grieving as moving through
predictable stages. In the following viewpoint, Drs. J. Trig Brown
and G. Alan Stoudemire describe this pattern of grief and explain
that any substantial deviation from this process can result in
pathological, or abnormal, grieving that may have serious consequences for the survivor's emotional and physical health.

As you read, consider the following questions:
1. What three stages do the authors describe as the normal
   grieving process?
2. What harmful consequences do the authors believe may
   happen to someone suffering from prolonged grieving?
3. What is distorted grief, according to Brown and
   Stoudemire?

J. Trig Brown and G. Alan Stoudemire, "Normal and Pathological Grief," *Journal of the
American Medical Association*, July 15, 1983, Vol. 250, No. 3, p. 378. Copyright 1983,
American Medical Association.

For grief concealed strangles the soul.

K. Burton

Each day physicians care for patients and members of patients' families who are in various stages of dealing with the emotional impact of personal losses. The emotional reaction to a loss, known as the grief process, usually follows a relatively predictable course. Under certain circumstances, however, pathological patterns of grieving may develop and these can have profoundly negative effects on patients' physical and emotional health. . . .

Normal Patterns of Grief

The grief process has a restitutive and psychologically adaptive function. During this process the survivor reorganizes his or her world without the deceased, gradually is released from previously established intense emotional ties to the loved one, and reinvests these emotional ties in new interests and persons. This psychological and social reorganization requires that the survivor accept the reality of the loss even though the emotional impact can be devastating. Feelings of despair, helplessness, protest, anger, and sadness are normal reactions to loss that occur during the bereavement period. After a time, the bereaved gradually comes to deal with these painful emotions and begins to psychologically and socially adjust to life without the deceased. Acceptance of the reality of the loss, full comprehension of its ramifications, and the painful process of emotionally detaching oneself from the deceased is referred to as "grief work."

The fact that uncomplicated grief has predictable manifestions associated with functional impairment for the survivors prompted G.L. Engle to view grief within a "disease model" framework. In this model, he likens bereavement to a wound and the grief process that follows to the healing necessary for the complete restoration of function. Whether one fully agrees with this model or not, it is apparent that the process of uncomplicated grief follows a relatively predictable pattern with distinctive symptoms, but with possible complications as well.

Various terms have been used to describe the grief process, but the experience is invariably described as occurring in phases; one phase gradually follows the next as the grief work is accomplished. The concept that grief has a phasic course is clinically helpful in determining whether a person's reaction to loss is progressing as expected or is absent, delayed, or distorted. In the Figure, which is compiled from the works of E. Lindemann, J. Bowlby, C.M. Parkes and M. Greenblatt, the process of uncomplicated grief is

17

pictured as an interwoven pattern of changing emotional states, somatic symptoms, thoughts, and motivational stages. The phases overlap, as do each of the components within the phases.

The Phases of Grief

Phase 1, SHOCK, begins immediately after the loss. It lasts one to 14 days and serves to protect the bereaved from experiencing the overwhelmingly painful reality of the loss too quickly or intensely. During this period, the survivor is often in a state of shock, or numbed disbelief. Somatic symptoms include crying, throat tightness, dysphagia, sighing respirations, chest tightness, nausea, and a sensation of abdominal emptiness. Patients may feel lost, dazed, stunned, helpless, immobilized, and disorganized in attempting to cope with the devastating impact of their loss. The shock phase is more pronounced if the death is sudden or unexpected. A similar phase can be experienced after a grave diagnosis is announced, even though the patient may still have many years to live.

Normal and Abnormal Grief

With normal grief you are able to work your way back to productive and near normal living, while with abnormal grief you develop a chronic state of psychological or physical symptoms that persist for an unreasonable period of time. . . .

One of the best ways to gauge abnormal emotional reactions is to observe a person's behavior a month or so after the death. Most people will be quite back to normal by that time. If physical and emotional symptoms persist, and if the person is unable to function effectively after a few weeks, it is a fairly specific indication that he should have some special help in meeting his problems of adjustment.

Edgar N. Jackson, *Concerning Death*, 1974.

In phase 2, PREOCCUPATION WITH THE DECEASED, the sense of unreality and disbelief decreases. Emotional "numbness" gives way to fully experiencing the painful sadness of the loss. Symptoms of this period include insomnia, fatigue, anhedonia, and anorexia. Crying spells persist. Most characteristic of this period is an intense, almost obsessive, preoccupation with the memory of the deceased. Every aspect of the past relationship is recalled and examined in detail. Past grievances, unresolved anger, neglects, guilt, and other unresolved conflicts are reexamined. Dreams of the dead may be intensely vivid. Transient hallucinatory episodes may occur in which the deceased's voice is heard, or strangers are mistakenly identified as the deceased. A general period of social withdrawal and introversion are also typical. This phase is usually well developed by three weeks and may persist for up to six months, but "recurrences" of these symptoms also may be activated on anniversaries of the death, birthdays of the deceased, wedding aniversaries, special holidays, and other important dates that remind the survivor of the deceased. These "anniversary reactions" involve a revitalization of emotional attachments to the deceased and may occur with some regularity for years, even in relatively uncomplicated grief reactions.

Phase 3, RESOLUTION, is heralded by the bereaved's becoming able to recall past events with sentimental pleasure and regaining interest in activities. New social contacts are gradually made and life is reorganized around new activities and interests. Crying spells, feelings of emptiness, and the longing for the dead may still occur, but tend to diminish in intensity and duration. Somatic symptoms and preoccupation with memories begin to wane. "Getting over" a death does not mean that sad and empty feelings are never evoked by the memory of the lost one, but rather that the survivor does not remain preoccupied with the deceased or restricted socially and psychologically as a result of the death. One author has poignantly remarked, "You really don't get over it; you get used to it." . . .

Pathological Grief

The grief process does not always follow a phasic course to an adaptive completion. Complications are evident when the manifestations of grief are absent, are of extreme intensity, are prolonged, develop into a prolonged major depression, or become distorted in some manner. . . .

Delayed Grief

A slight delay in the grieving process may be normal, but a protracted delay or absent grief is a manifestation that the emotions experienced are so painful that they are being avoided at all costs. These individuals are often viewed by the community or family as coping well because they did not "break down and fall apart." The cost of delayed or absent grief is that these persons may suddenly experience symptoms of acute grief at anniversary dates, milestones, or following subsequent relatively minor losses. An alternate manifestation of unresolved grief is emotional numbing in which the patient may largely deny an emotional reaction to the loss. Some patients may experience many of the symptoms of a major depression (sleep disturbance, anorexia, weight loss, psychomotor retardation, or constricted affect) but largely deny that they feel particularly sad or despondent. Patients who experience persistent symptoms of a major depression, often with the development of coincidental unusual physical symptoms, should be carefully considered as having an unresolved or latent grief reaction. Often, the presence of unusual somatic symptoms

19

Phases of Uncomplicated Grief

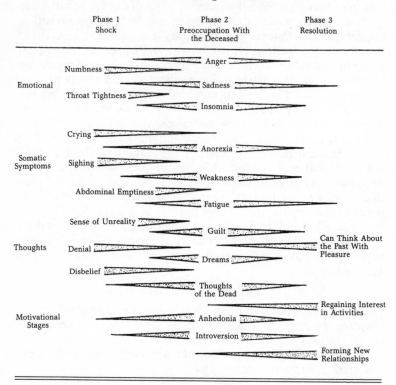

	Phase 1 Shock	Phase 2 Preoccupation With the Deceased	Phase 3 Resolution

may be the best clue to a "masked" depression that is the sequela of a delayed or absent grief process.

Grief reactions may be delayed by persistent denial of the reality of the death. This process often occurs when the body is never recovered, is destroyed, or mutilated, or is decomposed to a degree in which positive identification is not possible. Such a situation may arise in wartime or in catastrophic accidents. Some authorities believe that being allowed to view the body confirms the reality of the loss, prevents denial, and ultimately facilitates the grieving process. The following case demonstrates a delayed grief reaction due to failure to recover a body during wartime.

CASE [1] — A 53-year-old woman with vague somatic complaints had an unrevealing workup for these symptoms. Psychiatric evaluation was requested. It became apparent that the patient had been seen around the tenth anniversary of her notification that her son had been shot down while flying in Vietnam. The son's body had never been recovered. Despite confirmatory evidence from observers that the plane had burst into flames and that there was no possibility of survival, she had maintained for many years that her son was still living. She had continued to keep her son's room "as it was" in hope that he would someday return home. She had never permitted a memorial service to be held for him.

Psychotherapy involved gentle but persistent confrontation of her denial and of the impossibility of her son's survival. Once her denial began to lessen, a fully developed grief reaction emerged, with all of its features. At the completion of treatment, she was finally able to accept the reality of her son's death. More than ten years after his disappearance, a memorial service was finally arranged. . . .

Distorted Grief

The second major form of pathological grief occurs when the manifestations of the grief process become distorted. Lindemann described these variants of the distorted grief reaction as follows: (1) persistent compulsive overactivity without a sense of loss; (2) identification with the deceased and acquisition of symptoms belonging to the last illness of the deceased (conversion symptoms); (3) deterioration of health in the survivors with the development of medical illness; (4) social isolation, withdrawal, or alienation; and (5) severe depression.

The clinical presentation of a patient with a pathological grief reaction often reflects elements from more than one of these variants. As discussed previously, extreme guilt and anger at the deceased are often at the core of a pathological reaction. . . .

Unresolved anger is often at the heart of a distorted grief reaction and can develop into a major depression, as the following case demonstrates.

CASE [2] — A 32-year-old man was referred by his primary physician for treatment of severe depression, suicidal ideation, and alcoholism. The patient dated the onset of his problems to the death of his wife 16 months earlier. Her death was the result of an automobile accident. Further discussion revealed that the accident had occurred following an argument in which the wife's affair with a close friend of the husband had been revealed. A violent argument ensued in which the husband told her to leave and never return. The wife, distraught and fearing physical harm to herself, fled to her car and drove away in a frantic state of mind. Probably secondary to her fear and disorganization she ran a red light, hit another vehicle, and was killed instantly. The husband, despite her death, remained extremely angry and hurt because of the wife's affair and felt as if he had never been able to resolve the matter with her. In addition, he felt guilty and responsible for her death because of their argument. Once these factors were identified, the patient was referred for psychotherapy and further treatment of his alcoholism.

Treatment of pathological grief often involves in-depth psychological exploration of the circumstances of the death and the survivor's feelings about the deceased. The psychotherapeutic

21

goal is to identify possible causes of the abnormal grief reaction and to reactivate the process so that it might be completed. Often the treatment of pathological grief requires referral to persons specially trained in the necessary techniques, thus emphasizing the importance of appropriate recognition. . . .

Once the causes of the distorted reactions are understood, many of these patients can be treated by their personal physician. Appropriate techniques involve identifying feelings associated with the loss, and allowing patients to express their sadness, anger, and guilt. Bringing latent anger and guilt to a conscious level of awareness enables the patient to deal with the conflicted feelings in a more realistic manner. Once the grieving process has been reactivated, its course needs to be facilitated and monitored to ensure complete resolution and successful adaptation to the future.

"It is becoming clear that there is no strict timetable for grieving."

Grief Does Not Follow a Predictable Pattern

Christopher Joyce

While millions of physicians and the public in general adhere to the theories that grief over the death of a loved one follows a predictable pattern, some studies have questioned these theories. In the following viewpoint, Christopher Joyce, a free-lance science writer in Washington, DC, quotes from these studies. He argues that there is really no predictable grieving pattern or timetable; suggesting that there is one does psychological damage to those who fall outside of it.

As you read, consider the following questions:

1. What is the common myth our society holds about grieving, according to the author?
2. What does the author believe is abnormal grief?
3. How does Joyce believe resolution of grief should be determined?

Christopher Joyce, "A Time for Grieving," *Psychology Today*, November 1984. Reprinted with permission from Psychology Today Magazine. Copyright © 1984 American Psychological Association.

A 40-year-old woman learns that her husband has died violently in a fire at a nightclub. She becomes extremely depressed, cries bitterly, says she doesn't want to live and is utterly dejected for three days. She fears she is losing her mind and tells her therapist of her painful preoccupation with memories of her husband.

Gradually, the woman begins to acknowledge that her husband will never return, and after 10 days she accepts the loss. She begins to talk about her husband's remarkable qualities and his deep devotion to her. She is briefly distressed by her growing attachment to her therapist, but then accepts that as a sign of her ability to fill the emotional gap left by her husband. Ever more active, she makes plans, renews her interest in French, resumes her job as a secretary and eases back into the mainstream of life.

This nameless woman's story has served for decades as a yardstick against which the grief of millions has been measured. It was set down in 1944 by psychiatrist Erich Lindemann of Massachusetts General Hospital as part of a study of 101 bereaved persons, including 13 survivors of the tragic 1942 fire in which 491 people died in Boston's Cocoanut Grove nightclub. Her reaction, he wrote in a now-famous article, "Symptomatology and Management of Acute Grief," was a model for successful readjustment.

The grief of Lindemann's "normal" subjects followed a set pattern: After the initial shock, the bereaved felt intense sadness, withdrew, protested the loss and then, within a year, resolved the grief. Lindemann suggested that these are the stages of grief work which, like through dark chambers, the bereaved passes upward toward the light of readjustment. Grief that deviates from this pattern, he suggested, is morbid or pathological.

No Timetable for Grief

Not so, says psychologist Stephen Goldston, director of the Office of Prevention at the National Institute of Mental Health. "There is a common myth in our society," he says, "that grief is something that dissipates quickly, and that after two weeks people should be able to get back to work and forget about it." In fact, he says, it is becoming clear that there is no strict timetable for grieving.

Gerald Koocher, associate professor of psychology at Harvard Medical School, agrees. Sadness, he explains, may continue for years, flaring up on anniversaries or significant dates.

Goldston and Koocher are among a growing number of mental-health professionals who are reexamining the "rules" of bereavement and grief. They credit Lindemann with highlighting the symptoms of grief, a subject rarely studied since Freud distin-

24

guished mourning from melancholy in 1917. But these professionals suspect that Lindemann may have erred in setting a strict timetable for grief and in his criteria for distinguishing normal from pathological grief.

A . . . study done by the Institute of Medicine (IOM) of the National Academy of Sciences concludes that bereavement is associated with measurable distress in everyone, but that the distress can range greatly in intensity and duration. A survivor's way of life commonly is disturbed for at least one year but may be affected for as long as three years. And there is tremendous variation in the way people react to bereavement. These reactions, the report says, cannot be neatly plotted in a series of well-defined stages, nor is the progression from the time of death to the resolution of bereavement likely to be in a straight line. There are a number of psychological, social and biological processes that interact and make it difficult to define a normal reaction to bereavement.

Grieving May Last Years

The feelings of grief last far longer than society in general allows. Even closest friends may expect us to be back to "normal" in a few weeks after a death. But living with loss is not so simple. The death of someone close may cause emotional pain and confusion for months or even years. Losing someone we love through death is one of the most traumatic of life's experiences. Acute grief affects several million people every year.

Nancy O'Connor, *Letting Go With Love*, 1984.

"When you lose someone you love, weird things happen. That's normal," Koocher says. "For example, if you are walking down the street and you think you see the person who died, is that a hallucination? Or you think you hear them speaking. These can be normal experiences. A lot of people have these symptoms."

No Single Standard

What's abnormal? "It could be defined in many ways—the degree of pain a person is experiencing, and whether it prevents that person from resuming normal activities," Koocher says. But, he adds, there is just too much individual variation, especially in reaction to different types of death, for there to be a single standard.

Arthur Kleinman, professor of psychiatry and medical anthropology at Harvard Medical School, says the particulars of grief may not be universal, and that mental-health professionals should be wary of pegging "deviant" labels on grieving behavior. In some societies, a death is a communal event, a time to reassert traditional values and to reintegrate a community. Our society, Kleinman and others assert, has abandoned many of the rituals and traditions that used to help people deal with the loss of a loved one.

Some pychologists, like Koocher, are inventing rituals. For example, he asked the parents of a child who died of cancer to write a letter to the child saying some of the things they felt that they should have said when the child was alive.

Psychiatrists Replacing Family

Abetting what some see as a drift away from ritual and tradition in our culture is the contraction of the family and its new mobility. Many psychologists say people seek them out because they have no one else to turn to. They have to fill the gap for those whose traditional family, community or religious ties no longer provide support in times of grief.

The IMO report says therapeutic intervention programs can help people move faster through the grieving process but admits that not all people want or need formal therapy. However, the report goes on, for people who continue to be overwhelmed by their grief or are unable to grieve, psychotherapeutic intervention may be necessary. In addition, certain categories of people may be at especially high risk for illness and even death. These include young children who have lost a parent or sibling, people with a history of psychiatric disorders (especially depression) and people related or close to someone who has committed suicide. More research is needed, the report suggests, to help in identifying people at risk and to determine which therapies are the most effective.

Formulating a New Theory

Few academics care to follow this line of research, and one reason may be because they are as "death-denying" as the rest of society, Goldston says. But some, like Koocher, have devoted a great deal of time to the study of death and bereavement. Koocher plans a five-year study of 300 bereaved families. Looking for objective signs such as illness or days missed from work or school, as well as subjective reports of grief, he hopes to formulate a new theory of grief. He also teaches the facts of death and bereavement to medical students—a group, he says, that normally gets little training in the subject.

John Spinetta, professor of psychology at San Diego State University, studies how families cope with the death of a child. He has followed the course of bereavement in 120 families in which children died of cancer, trying to pinpoint the traits that distinguish the families that bounce back quickly from those that languish in grief. Although he still can't predict into which camp a family will fall, he has developed a scale to measure how well a family is doing after the death of a child. He asks whether the family can talk about or see reminders of the child without shedding tears. Are they making plans? Have they returned to "normal" activities, like jobs, clubs, hobbies? Are they filled with continuing questions about why it happened?

The Best Way To Help

Through these and other ongoing studies, mental-health researchers hope not only to redefine normal grieving behavior but to learn what behavioral signs among the bereaved signal a need for special help. Although many gaps exist in our understanding of the bereavement process, the IOM study concludes, it is time to put the puzzle together and to determine the best way to help people who have lost someone with whom they have had close emotional ties.

"Let your heart break. Let go of the suffering that keeps you back from life."

Cope with Death by Openly Grieving

Stephen Levine

Stephen Levine has for several years counseled the terminally ill. He has worked with Elisabeth Kübler-Ross and for seven years directed the Hanumna Dying Project. A consultant to a number of hospice, hospital, and mediation groups, he is the co-author of *A Gradual Awakening* and *Who Dies?* The following viewpoint is excerpted from his book *Meetings at the Edge*, which consists of a series of dialogues between his patients and himself. In this selection, the author describes a woman, Dorothy, who is having a difficult time dealing with her young daughter's impending death. Levine suggests she openly grieve for her daughter, which in turn helps resolve both her daughter's fear and her own reluctance to accept death.

As you read, consider the following questions:

1. Why does the author discourage Dorothy from hiding her feelings from her daughter?
2. What suggestions does Levine give to Dorothy?
3. How does the grieving process bring Dorothy closer to her daughter, according to the author?

Excerpts from MEETINGS AT THE EDGE by Stephen Levine. Copyright © 1984 by Stephen Levine. Reprinted by permission of Doubleday & Company, Inc.

Dorothy called one morning to say that her nine-year-old daughter was dying of lymphoma. After an unexpected, six-week illness the lymph nodes had begun "popping up like popcorn," to which she added, "It feels to me and to the doctors as if it is already a bit too late for any sort of intervention."

S: "Does you daughter understand what is happening to her?"
D: "No, not entirely. She asked me the other day, 'Mom, I am really pretty sick, aren't I?' and I said, 'Little girls nine years old don't usually get so lumpy.' "

Her mother added, "We will take it quiet now and do the things we are able to do. She has been out of school but I have not pressed it. She asked me what they were running the test for and I said cancer. And she said, 'People die with that, don't they?' And I said, 'Certainly they die with that and they also die crossing the streets.' I tried to be very casual with her."

I asked Dorothy if she thought her fear at that moment may have caused her to miss a moment of truth. If indeed her daughter wasn't trying to see past the barrier of Dorothy's motherhood and protection to some place essential where she could share her fears and her confusion of what she was moving toward.

D: "At this point, as long as she is active, I am not going to say much of what is happening. The night before last two lymph nodes in her groin began swelling and one on her neck about three days before that. And she said, 'Why am I getting these, Mom?' "

I mentioned to Dorothy that she sounded very matter-of-fact. That rather than holding back, as painful as it might be, perhaps she might investigate more deeply what she felt, and I asked her, "What if your daughter died tonight? What would remain unsaid? What have you not shared with her that you might wish to?" To which she replied, "At first I cried at night, but in the days I try to deal with it objectively." I pointed out that her daughter only saw her during the day, however; that her daughter might benefit from sharing in some of those tears so she might see some of the softness that her mother felt at night when they were both apart. Dorothy said, "I decided not to go through all that."

Deciding on Feeling

S: "Do you think emotions are something you can just decide about?"
D: "To a large extent, yes, at least the display of them."
S: "What seems inappropriate about sharing your concern?"
D: "At this point I would just like to try and remain as normal

29

as humanly possible."

S: "What do you mean by normal? Isn't the sharing of this grief normal under the circumstances? Mightn't it open a deeper contact between you two, a healing of the confusion and isolation which is frightening to you both? Truly, you can't go through the door with her, but you can accompany her more fully to the threshold."

D: "I have felt so alone for the past weeks and I guess she must too. I have lost so much in life. My husband died of cancer three years ago. I have lost two other children to cancer as well. There is so much grief, I don't know where to start. I think basically we are always alone. I don't like it but I don't know what to do about it."

S: "You have pushed so much away that now it seems impossible to make room for it all, but that is your daughter's legacy to you. Each grief demands to be recognized—the pain around your heart is its voice. Can you feel that sensation in the middle of your chest over your heart?"

D: "No."

S: "No soreness?"

D: "Well, yes."

Open Grief at a Father's Grave

"Then my legs folded under me," she writes, "and I sat down in the sopping grass. I couldn't understand why I was crying so hard.

"Then I remembered that I had never cried for my father's death.

"My mother hadn't cried either. She had just smiled and said what a merciful thing it was for him that he had died, because if he had lived he would have been crippled and an invalid for life, and he couldn't have stood that, he would rather have died than had that happen.

"I laid my face to the smooth face of the marble and howled my loss into the cold salt rain."

Sylvia Plath, *The Bell Jar*, 1962.

I explored with Dorothy that she might find a quiet place in the house some evening and start to focus on that sensation in the center of her chest. To start to open to whatever pain arose there because the heart armors itself, and her work now is to allow her heart to be torn open to the truths of the present moment. Focusing on the sensation, she might find that it would become very distinct and that she could start breathing directly into it as though it were a vent opening into her heart. That the soreness was the touch point of her heart, and as she entered this great soreness of heart all sorts of associated images might arise in the mind, glimpses of the deaths of others and the hard swallowing of long-held tears. To open to this fear and notice how it forms a shell around each stiff breath. To meet this fear with a willingness to be in this pain as a means of going beyond it into the vast love just beneath. If she wished her heart to touch her daughter's heart, she must focus on whatever old grief and broken longings blocked that touch point. I shared with her that this was not a time to seek safe territory as obviously there was no way she could protect her daughter from the experience of this time. All she could do was open in love to these precious moments that remained.

S: "How merciless we are with ourselves. How little we are available to ourselves and to others when we are maintaining this sort of self-protection which we have been told to cultivate our whole life through. Indeed, your daughter's teaching for you may be to start to tune in to the suffering which has so long been present in your heart. But by pulling back, as you have so many times in the past, you may find just another dark veil drawn across the heart, another moment missed that you wish to share with your daughter. I know it is a tough one."

Childhood Memories of Death

Dorothy shared with me her fear of opening to those feelings. "When I was a child, I was given a puppy for Christmas, a little cocker spaniel. He was like one of my dolls—but better—he was alive—but he got run over two months later and that same week my grandmother died—no one wanted to hear about my puppy and we weren't allowed to talk about Grandma. I guess I just didn't know what to do with it all—something in me shut down, I guess. I've put each death in my life behind me as quickly as possible. I almost never cry. I would like to get out all this grief but it sounds like such a bummer."

S: "How much more of a bummer is it to feel cut off from the world? From your daughter at a time of such need? We keep guarding our heart—we want to be so together, and in being so together we retract from the world into a kind of drowsy blindness that lets life slip by unshared."

D: "But it has always seemed so much safer to hold back from all this pain."

"Let Your Heart Break"

S: "That is what we have so often been encouraged to do. But you know, it is pretty hard to kiss someone who is keeping a stiff upper lip. How does this stiffness feel? Does it leave you sore all over? Where is the safety? You can't keep from dying, you can't keep your heart from aching—the pain just becomes more unbearable, seemingly unworkable. You have to do exactly what

31

you wish your daughter to do right now—to open, to soften around the pain, to make contact with something essential. All the holding back of a lifetime has become focused now in this predicament. It is time to be kind to yourself, to use these days or weeks as a deepening of your opening to life—by just loving her and being with her as your heart allows.

"As we speak now, just close your eyes and gently move into the pain. Allow the heart's armoring to melt. There is a vastness you share with your daughter. An edgeless unity with her, and all that is, which can be discovered when the heart allows itself to be torn open. Allow the pain to penetrate into the very center of your heart. Let go of any resistance that falsely assures you it is your only defense. Share in the deathlessness of just being in the moment, with whatever it offers. Allowing yourself to go beyond the defenses of the mind. Move into the very heart of the moment. It can allow an experience of much greater context than the fearful attachment to the body. This is the unfinished work we are so frightened to move into. Clearly death is not the enemy. It is our lack of self-trust. Our forgetfulness of the extraordinary nature which inhabits this tiny body for a moment. I don't mean just your daughter's tiny body. I mean your tiny body as well. Go gently through without force. Just opening a moment at a time to the feelings and pain that arise there in the middle of your chest. With great kindness to yourself, remember how force, again and again, closes the heart."

D: "You know, even though my mind is fighting against what you are saying, the sensation in my heart is beginning to make me feel like my heart will burst. I just want to cry."

S: "Good. Let your heart break. Let go of the suffering that keeps you back from life. Do you hear yourself now? Your heart is so open and the pain is right there. You are doing now just what you need to do—to just feel with so much compassion for yourself what you are going through.

"There is no rush to this process of opening, there is no emergency. Just slowly begin to make room in your heart for yourself. Perhaps tonight you will sit down with your daughter and feel that pain and just share it with her."

Feeling the Pain

We spoke of the resistance to life which filters every perception, which pushes away our connectedness with all that we love and leaves us feeling so isolated. And I encouraged her to just start to breathe in to her heart with whatever love might mean to her at that moment and to breath it back out, to send it to her daughter. To allow herself to move into her experience and not hold back. That her essential connectedness with her daughter would become apparent beyond the ancient barricades which had so often kept her separate from the moment. "Let your pain be there and open

32

around it. Open so that you can feel her pain and your pain together. You know, if pain made a sound, the atmosphere would be humming all the time. What you are sharing with your daughter now is being shared by tens of thousands of other beings at this very moment. Let it be in love instead of fear. Let her death be surrounded by your care for her and a willingness to go beyond your fear. To open to her death in a kind of new birth shared now for you both."

D: "I can't talk much now, my chest hurts so, but in my heart I hear my daughter saying 'thank you.' "

Before Dorothy's daughter died, they had many long "midnight talks" about her father's and brother's deaths. Dorothy said at first she was "terribly uncomfortable bringing this all up" but that it seemed to put her daughter more at ease. "We talked at length about cancer and God. And I told her I loved her in a way that even losing her could not diminish. I don't think I have ever acknowledged my feelings to anyone so directly. It felt terrible. It felt wonderful."

"We must take care not to formalize or prescribe the way in which people express emotion."

Open Grieving May Not Be Necessary

Norman Klein

Norman Klein is associate professor of anthropology at California State University in Los Angeles. In the following viewpoint, Klein expresses his belief that current theories place excessive emphasis on the grieving process. Different cultures and individuals react differently to death, he argues, and society should not place a single standard on how to grieve.

As you read, consider the following questions:

1. What "faddish" therapies does the author describe for resolving grief? What does he think is wrong with them?
2. What differences does the author see in the way cultural groups react to death?
3. What does the author believe are the new myths and stereotypes of death?

Norman Klein, "Is There a Right Way To Die?" October, 1978. Reprinted from *Psychology Today Magazine.* Copyright © 1978 Zidd-Davis Publishing Company.

In our own society, faddish therapies stress the idea that openly expressing sorrow, anger, or pain is a good thing, and the only means for "dealing with one's feelings honestly." "Holding things in" comes to be seen as deviant.

Yet nowhere has it been convincingly proved that expressing grief has universal therapeutic value. Perhaps more important, this insistence on the requirement to feel and tell represents an ethnocentric standard that can do injustice to persons and groups who cope differently.

Grief and Denial

Americans are said to fear and deny death, and if the denial becomes complete, it requires "defenses which can only be destructive," in the words of Elisabeth Kübler-Ross. She is perhaps best known for her scheme of the five stages of a "complete" death: (1) denial, (2) anger, (3) bargaining, (4) depression, and (5) acceptance. Each stage has a transitional value—taken alone, for instance, denial is seen as bad, though as a temporary buffer it is good—and, given enough time, a patient can reach a point of accepting death.

Kübler-Ross's work is undoubtedly useful; it may even help family, friends, and professionals to assist the dying patient who has the emotional needs she describes.

Yet it is surely conceivable that some Americans can work through grief internally or privately, without psychological cost; it is even more conceivable that whole cultural subgroups may have different ways of conceiving and responding to such experience. Harvard psychiatrist Ned H. Cassem has questioned the generally negative view of denial espoused by Kübler-Ross. "Denial can be a constructive force, enabling people to put out of mind morbid, frightening, and depressing aspects of life."

Standards May Be Arbitrary

A cross-cultural perspective reveals how arbitrary any one such standard may be. In 1976, psychologists Paul Rosenblatt, Patricia Walsh, and Douglas Jackson used the Human Relations Area Files, a massive compendium of anthropological data, to examine mourning in a large number of societies. They found in their review of 73 societies that what varies is the form and intensity of its expression. In 72 societies, people weep at death; the Balinese say they laugh to avoid crying. Are the Balinese unhealthy?

The researchers also correlated gender differences in crying for 60 societies: in 32 of them, both sexes cried equally; in the 28 in which there was a difference, it was always the women who cried more. Are they healthier?

In 18 of 32 societies, self-injury (such as cutting off a finger at a joint) is regularly attempted by both grieving men and women; women self-mutilate more in 12. But if emotional letting go is a good thing, should men and women, equally, mutilate themselves even more frequently?

Comparing Ethnic Values

Closer to home, psychologist Richard Kalish and anthropologist David Reynolds compared the attitudes on death and mourning of black Americans, Japanese-Americans, Mexican-Americans, and white Americans in Los Angeles. Asked if they would "try very hard to control the way you showed your emotions in public," the groups offered a wide range of responses. Japanese and black respondents said they would (82 percent, 79 percent) more often than white Americans and Mexican-Americans, for example (74 percent, 64 percent).

Japanese-Americans, who are most frequently reticent about public grief, would seem to bear out the stereotypic notion of Orientals as stoic. Public-health nurse Thelma Dobbins Payne reports that the reluctance of many Japanese-American women to cry out during childbirth leads some non-Japanese physicians to "wonder if Japanese women feel the pain." Japanese-American physicians, however, described a common alternative style in labor: "wincing," "grimacing," "frowning."

How much and what type of emoting is necessary to avoid the label "stoic"? The real issue rests with the way the various cultures define the appropriate expression of emotion. At the same time, it is very important to note that in no group Kalish and Reynolds studied was there a 100 percent agreement by all informants—sex, age, religion, and education all affected the responses.

The Jargon of Concern

"Death with dignity" and "a beautiful death" verge on becoming the new jargon of concern. But for whom are these expressions really meaningful? Do they describe the dying person's experience, or the observer's? Attitudes toward death are clearly influenced by culture—and by subculture, and by individual personality. It follows, then, that we must take care not to formalize or prescribe the way in which people express emotion. As Kalish and Reynolds remark in their discussion, "This era is in danger of replacing old myths and stereotypes with new myths and stereotypes, slightly more accurate and less destructive perhaps, but nonetheless not always appropriate."

"A sincere expression of caring—and sharing— can help us to turn the grief of futility and despair into the grief of faith and hope and release."

Friends Can Help the Grieving Cope with Death

Barbara Russell Chesser

Hearing of a friend's or relative's loss sends many people into an agonizing dilemma of their own. Not wishing to offend the grieving person, friends may avoid the situation, fearing that what they say or do could be the wrong thing. In the following viewpoint, Barbara Russell Chesser, a writer, insists that virtually anything a friend does will help the grieving person. She writes that there are five concrete things a friend can do to help.

As you read, consider the following questions:

1. Why does Chesser believe it is important for the grieving person to see and hear from friends?
2. What does the author mean when she says friends should listen to the grieving person?
3. What, according to Chesser, is the one *wrong* thing a friend can say to a grieving person?

Barbara Russell Chesser, "How to Comfort Those Who Grieve," *Reader's Digest*, April 1986. Reprinted with the author's permission.

The phone call came like a hammer blow. "Both of Gail Simone's parents were killed last night in a car crash." The caller was W.J. Wimpee, chaplain of Baylor University in Waco, Texas. He knew that Gail, a student, was a friend of mine. When I heard what had happened, a terrible numbness set in. *What can I do to help?*

This age-old question arises whenever a relative, friend or colleague suffers a death in the family. Like me that day, most people are at a loss to know how to respond. Trying to find some answers, I later talked with Chaplain Wimpee.

"Many people are immobilized out of fear they'll do or say the wrong thing," he said. Obviously, there is no one dramatic gesture or pearl of wisdom that will dissolve the heartache, but there are many acts of thoughtfulness that can convey your concern and help to soften the blow that a friend or loved one has suffered. From Wimpee and other experts on bereavement, here are five ways to say "I care."

1. Be there. Fran Philips was a real-estate agent in New York City. During an especially busy winter period, Fran's mother died. The funeral was to be held in Bel Air, Md., that weekend, and Helen, Fran's boss, would have to handle Fran's work on top of her own.

Helen was warmly sympathetic, and insisted that Fran leave for Bel Air right away. Heavy snows were forecast. "If you hurry," Helen said, "you might beat the weather."

Two days later, as Fran was greeting her mother's friends after services at the chapel, Helen came up quietly behind her. She had driven all night through a snowstorm. "Why stay in New York," Helen asked, "when all my thoughts were here with you?"

Going to the Funeral

For years, Chuck Grayson, an insurance man in Lexington, Ky., avoided funerals. "I didn't think it made much difference whether I went or not," he recalls. "But when my wife died, I saw how many friends and relatives made a special effort to be at her funeral. Suddenly I knew how important this is to the person who has suffered the loss."

It is just as important to go to the bereaved person's home. "I don't remember anything that was said," my mother recalls of the period after my father died, when well-wishers flocked to her home. "What I *do* remember are those heartfelt hugs."

By being there, you can help in other ways. John DeFrain, a social researcher at the University of Nebraska, has studied about 500 families who have experienced unexpected death. "At first," he says, "they are so stunned they don't even know what *they* need to do, let alone tell others how to help." This is why people who are grief-struck seldom respond to the well-meaning offer, "if there is anything I can do, let me know."

A Letter to a Friend

Please dear friend
Don't say to me the old clichés
Time heals all wounds
God only gives you as much as you can bear
Life is for the living. . .
Just say the thoughts of your heart
I'm sorry, I love you, I'm here, I care
Hug me and squeeze my hand
I need your warmth and strength.

Please don't drop your eyes when I am near
I feel so rejected now by God and man
Just look in my eyes and let me know that you are with me.

Don't think you must always be strong for me
It's okay to cry
It tells me how much you care
Let me cry, too
It's so lonely to always cry alone.

Please keep coming by even after many weeks have passed
When the numbness wears off the pain of grief is unbearable.
Don't ever expect me to be quite the same
How can I be when part of my being is here no more.

But please know, dear friend, with your love, support and understanding
I will live and love again and be grateful everyday
                              that I have you—dear friend.

Mary Bailey

Elaine Vail, *A Personal Guide to Living with Loss.* New York: John Wiley & Sons, 1982. Reprinted with permission.

Even a government agency like NASA recognizes the importance of being there. Following the fire and explosion that destroyed the *Challenger* space shuttle in January [1986], the families of each of the seven astronauts who were lost had another astronaut family at their side soon after the disaster. The support families were there to help the *Challenger* families with everything from travel and food arrangements to boarding the family pet. "With the vast technology of our space age," says Clarke Covington, manager of the Space-Station Project at NASA's Johnson Space Center in Houston, "there's still nothing more powerful than one human being reaching out to another."

2. Listen. "One month after their high-school graduation, two boys were killed in an accident," says Bob Johns, youth pastor of a church in Woodway, Texas. "I visited both sets of parents, and we talked about the weather, our jobs—everything but their sons." Johns had felt he should never intrude on privacy and grief.

Then he heard a speaker from Compassionate Friends, a national organization that helps parents cope with the death of a child. The speaker's son had died. "She said no one would talk about him. Her greatest fear was that her son's short life would go unnoticed and unremembered." Johns began to realize that grieving people need to talk about this sudden vacuum in their lives.

A short time later, Johns encountered the father of one of the boys killed in the accident. After the usual amenities, Johns said, "Scott and I had a wonderful visit the last time I saw him." Immediately, the father's face lit up. "Really? What did he say?" Johns recounted their last conversation. "Then Scott's father started talking," says Johns, "and it was like a floodgate opening up."

What Not To Say

In a survey of bereaved people, 20 out of 25 felt most sympathizing comments didn't help and some actually hurt. Cited were such remarks as: "It's better now because he is at peace"; "Don't question God's purpose"; "You'll get over this." Above all, never say, "I know how you feel" unless you really have gone through the same experience.

The best way to get a mourner to open up is with a question: "Would you like to talk?" or "It must be hard to think about life without her; how are you adjusting?"

The need to listen and show grief extends to children, says Catherine Loughlin, retired professor of child development at the University of Nevada in Reno. When her husband died suddenly, their son, Martin, was six and daughter, Louise, only three. Loughlin said little to them about their father and returned to normal family routine as soon as possible. About six months later, Louise blurted, "Won't Daddy be surprised when he sees how I've grown!" Martin wrinkled his young brow. "Daddy is dead. Let's not talk about him ever again!"

Catherine Loughlin realized her children had been wrestling with the same painful emotions that she had been stifling. "When we began sharing our feelings," she says, "we finally began to accept the unacceptable."

3. Send a note. Julie, an honor student at the University of Nebraska and the only daughter of Clark and June Hudson, was hit by a truck and died. The Hudsons cherish a note from one of Julie's professors. "She wrote us," June says, "how much she had enjoyed having Julie in class, how cheerful and considerate she was and how much others liked her. It eased our misery to know that she was remembered that way."

Notes can share personal memories or they can be simple and short, such as "I'm thinking of you during these painful days," or "I am praying for you during this time."

One of my friends wrote simply, "My prayer for you is a verse which meant a lot to me when my daughter died: 'Cast your burden on the Lord, and he will sustain you.'" (Psalm 55:22)

4. Give a gift. After Mary Christensen's 19-year-old daughter was killed in a motorcycle and car collision in Connecticut, she found solice in a collection of poems that a friend gave her. "She took special care in choosing something that would be meaningful to me," Mary says. "The poems put into words all the emotions I was feeling."

Helping Our Friends

The help of loving and supportive friends can be immensely valuable in the long and painful process of trying to build a new life without that special person whose loss seems insurmountable. But because we feel uneasy around those who are grieving, we usually spend less time with them at the precise period in their lives when they need us most. . . .

We can become a very useful and significant source of comfort for our friends who are bereaved. In our often fruitless search for the right thing to say, we frequently forget that there are lots of things that we can *do* to help our friends through a period of mourning and readjustment.

Elizabeth Ogg, *Facing Death and Loss,* 1985.

For years our neighbors had admired the beautiful flowers my grandfather grew. When he died, the neighbors gave the community library a book on flowering plants, in memory of Granddad. My grandmother was deeply moved.

Useful Books

Several widows I know received Helen Thames Raley's book *For Those Who Wait for Morning: Thoughts on Being a Widow* soon after their husbands died; and they, in turn, give the book to other new widows. *Tracks of a Fellow Struggler,* by John Claypool, may be helpful to parents who have lost a child. Other books that console include *When Bad Things Happen to Good People,* by Rabbi Harold Kushner; and *Don't Take My Grief Away,* by Doug Manning.

5. Extend an invitation. Kim Parker's mother died the summer Kim turned 17. "It was one week before my birthday," she recalls. "At the end of every summer, Mom and I had always combined my birthday with shopping for school clothes. It was our special day together." Kim's friend Cari knew this. "So on the morning of the first birthday after my mother died," Kim says, "Cari called and asked if I would like to go shopping for school clothes. This was the most thoughtful thing anyone could have done."

An invitation gives the bereaved something to look forward to—instead of looking back on the source of pain and suffering. Consider what the person likes to do: Eat out? Go to plays? Take a drive? A friend of mine remembers that during the first few days after her husband's funeral, even a simple trip to the supermarket was difficult. "Now I always ask a new widow to let me go with her to the grocery store," she says.

Bereaved people often decline invitations—or accept only to cancel at the last minute. "People in deep mourning may fear losing control of their emotions in front of others," says Paul Stripling, executive director of the Waco Baptist Association. "They may even feel that if they have a good time, they are being disloyal to the person's memory." Gentle encouragement, he says, "will help them know it's all right to begin enjoying life again."

The death of a loved one is a devastating emotional loss. But a sincere expression of caring—and sharing—can help us to turn the grief of futility and despair into the grief of faith and hope and release.

"Another mother who had lost a baby would know what she was feeling."

Fellow Sufferers Can Help the Grieving

Judy Sklar Rasminsky

Grieving for the loss of a loved one, says Judy Sklar Rasminsky, can be a lonely process. While one is enmeshed in feelings of loss and pain, the world goes on as though nothing has happened. This discrepancy can cause the grieving person to become seriously depressed. In the following viewpoint, Rasminsky relates the story of Sandi Greeley whose baby died at birth. Greeley had the opportunity to speak with other mothers who had also lost their babies. Being with these women allowed Sandi to express her grief openly, and reassured her that it would pass.

As you read, consider the following questions:

1. Why was Sandi reassured when the other mother spoke with her?
2. Why do you think Sandi decided to become a counselor?

Judy Sklar Rasminsky, "When a Baby Dies," *Reader's Digest*, April 1984. Reprinted with the author's permission.

Sandi Greeley, 30 years old and eight months pregnant, lay wide awake and rigid with fear in the early-morning hours. She was in labor, but the contractions weren't coming fast enough to warrant leaving for the hospital. So she waited in the Greeleys' neat little brick-and-frame house in a St. Louis suburb. Waited not just for more frequent contractions but to feel her baby kick inside her. (For months they had called the baby Derek, certain he was a boy.)

Sandi had not felt Derek move since she'd had a minor car accident eight hours before. Though doctors who checked Sandi at the emergency room had heard the baby's heartbeat, she couldn't rid herself of worry. She kneaded her stomach, pleading, "Move, Derek! Do something."

At last she woke her husband, Jim. "Something's wrong," she said. "Let's get to the hospital."

Sandi's obstetrician, Dr. Fred Johnson, met them there. Moving the fetal stethoscope slowly over her stomach, he listened carefully. At last he turned it off and said, "Sandi, I'm sorry." The baby was dead.

They Wanted *That* Baby

It was Friday, August 6, 1976, one month and two days before Sandi's due date. Sandi and Jim had wanted this baby so much. The would never have one now, they agreed. They couldn't go through this agony a third time. It had been so awful after the miscarriage two years ago. They had felt such pain, yet no one seemed to understand what that baby had meant to them. Even family members had said, "It's only a miscarriage. You'll have another baby." But they had wanted *that* baby. Now, after eight months of planning for Derek's arrival, he wouldn't be there either. Jim and Sandi clung to each other on the narrow hospital bed and wept.

For Sandi's health and the safety of future pregnancies, Dr. Johnson wanted her to go through labor. Since her contractions had stopped, the Greeleys went home to wait—and grieve.

Later that morning they began the difficult task of telling their family and friends. Janet Wittenauer, a neighbor, was hanging wash when Jim came into her yard. "The baby died," he said, tears in his eyes. Janet came to see Sandi in the afternoon. "Some of the women in a group I belong to have lost babies, like you," Janet said. "They formed an organization to help one another out. Would you like to talk to one of them?"

Sandi was surprised. She knew that Janet was an active member

of Life Seekers, an organization of St. Louis women who raise
funds to save the lives of critically ill newborns. But she had never
heard of A.M.E.N.D. (Aiding Mothers Experiencing Neonatal
Death). Surely another mother who had lost a baby would know
what she was feeling.

The call came that evening. "This is Judie Constantino. I lost
a baby too, and I've been trained to help other mothers cope with
a miscarriage, a neonatal death, or a stillbirth like yours."

Sandi made a date for Judie to come over Monday, but the visit
had to be postponed when Sandi went into labor on Sunday night.
Monday morning the baby was delivered. Neither of the parents
ever saw Derek, but Sandi pictured him in her mind as a chubby
blond, and her arms ached with loneliness.

Another Mother's Invaluable Advice

The best advice I ever got came from two other mothers. One, an
early acquaintance at the hospital, had a child that frankly disturbed
me. She was the essence of death, a virtual skeleton. Every
unpleasantness that can happen to a cancer patient had happened
to this child. . . .

She [M.] was an agonizing reminder of what might happen to my
beautiful little girl, and I was very uncomfortable around her. . . .

The morning M. died, we somehow missed the news. As her mother
was leaving the hospital for the last time, she came into our room,
took my hands in hers, and said, "Good luck to you."

Instantly I knew, and I was afraid. M. was the first. So kids really
did die here.

We stepped into the hall, and she said, "Don't be afraid to let her
go." We embraced, and she went away, leaving me with that simple but weighty philosophy. And it was an invaluable legacy.

Martha Pearse Elliott, *Living with Death and Dying*, 1981.

Judie, the mother of two young boys, came to visit the following Monday. Sandi asked immediately about the death of Judie's
baby. Judie told her briefly and then said, "But each experience
is unique, and although we feel many of the same feelings, each
of us reacts differently and has different ways of coping. Tell me
about your baby. How did he die?"

"They don't know exactly," Sandi said. She told Judie about the
car accident. "I keep thinking about it, wondering if I killed him.
I feel so guilty. If only I hadn't driven. . . . "

"I'm sure it wasn't your fault," Judie said. "The doctors heard
his heartbeat after the accident. Maybe after they've examined
the placenta they'll have a better idea of what happened. Write
down all your questions and have a long talk with Dr. Johnson."

45

Judie doesn't seem to have any answers, Sandi thought. *Yet I'm beginning to feel a little better. She really hears what I say.*

"Judie, when will it stop hurting? Will I ever stop crying?"

"In time," Judie said. "But remember, you've lost a very important person in your life. He's worth grieving for, the same way you would cry for your parents or for Jim. Don't be afraid to talk to Jim about what you feel. That will help."

Sandi cried with relief when Judie left. She had been told that her feelings—the anger, the depression, the fear she was going crazy—were all normal. The grief she and Jim were having would pass, and maybe they would try to have another baby after all, an idea that had seemed impossible two hours before.

Visiting the Grave

Judie had said it might help to visit Derek's grave. Bringing daisies, Sandi and Jim went to the cemetery in September. They cried and then wandered around reading the dates on other small headstones, feeling less alone. . . .

The brightest spot in Sandi's life soon became Life Seekers, A.M.E.N.D.'s parent organization. She volunteered to do secretarial work—the first step she'd taken into the world since Derek's death. In the back of her mind was the idea that eventually she would be an A.M.E.N.D. counselor, but first she had to resolve her grief and successfully have another child.

Sandi's sister Cheryl, eight years her junior, had been five months pregnant with her first child when Derek died. On December 18, Sandi's mother phoned. "Cheryl had a boy," she said.

It took Sandi three weeks to summon the courage to visit Cheryl and her son, Joshua. But when the baby got pneumonia, Sandi told Judie, "I don't want her to lose that baby!" The sisters found a new rapport that endured after Joshua recovered.

How Long Will I Grieve?

With spring's arrival, Sandi's "down" days were fewer, but the emotions were still there, waiting to be triggered. In April Sandi went to watch Jim play softball. Among the other wives and children, there were three babies born over the winter. She felt the pain all over again and wandered slowly to another field to collect herself. Later she phoned Judie. "How long will this go on?" she asked.

"A year is perfectly normal," Judie reminded her. "Even five years from now when you see children getting on the school bus to go to kindergarten, you may think about how Derek should be with them."

By June the world looked remarkably different: Sandi was pregnant. And to everyone's surprise and delight, the pregnancy was practically trouble-free. On February 15, 1978, six-pound two-ounce Valerie Dawn Greeley came into the world.

Now a mother, Sandi signed up for A.M.E.N.D. training in the summer. During the six three-hour sessions run by professional psychotherapists Louise Felts and Jacquelyn Wheeler, she formed strong bonds with the other seven trainees. As they exchanged stories of their losses, reactions and ways of coping, each woman, so seemingly under control, revealed a part of herself that was not healed.

Sandi learned that the other mothers had seen and even held their babies who died. She ardently wished that she had been surer of herself when Derek was being delivered. She told the group, "If it happened tomorrow, I would make sure I saw my baby. I never got to say hello, and I never got to say good-by."

In a discussion about grief, Sandi told the group how, when their baby died, her husband would answer the phone, and people would say, "How is Sandi?" Nobody ever asked how he was. "One night," Sandi said, "he just had more than he could handle. He got off the phone and cried. 'Everyone asks how *you* feel,' he said. 'But nobody ever asks *me*. Doesn't anyone realize that I'm the father of this baby?' " Sandi's story eventually became a standard part of A.M.E.N.D.'s instruction.

Feeling the Same Pain

Who then can so softly bind up the wound of another as he who has felt the same wound himself?

Thomas Jefferson, *Letter to Maria Cosway.*

After Sandi's training was completed, her group joined the other counselors, who meet each month to discuss their cases with Felts and Wheeler. When Sandi had been to two meetings, Maureen Connelly, the group's coordinator, phoned her. "I have a mother for you," she said.

Scared to death, but ready to listen as intently and compassionately as Judie had listened to her, Sandi dialed the number. "My name is Sandi Greeley," she said. "I'm your A.M.E.N.D. counselor, and I lost a baby too. Would you like to talk about the death of your baby?"

Sandi, who counseled 13 mothers over the next five years, is now the mother of three girls. Emily Kathleen, a chubby blonde, was born on February 27, 1980. And on December 30, 1982, Laurie Elizabeth joined the Greeley family.

Write Your Own Epitaph

An epitaph is a brief statement (often found on a tombstone) in remembrance of a dead person. It usually tries to express in a few words what was significant or memorable about the person's life. This activity will give you a chance to write an epitaph for yourself and for others. It will allow you to think about who you are and how you would like to be remembered.

Step 1

Read the epitaphs listed on the following pages. Choose two epitaphs that you believe give the clearest picture of what the persons were really like. Next, choose the two epitaphs you enjoy the most. Why do you enjoy them?

Step 2

Write an epitaph for each of the following. Each epitaph should be one to three sentences in length. Remember that if someone were to read these epitaphs a hundred years from now, this is all they would know about these people.

1. For yourself
2. For a classmate
3. For a famous public figure—this includes
   political leaders, actors, artists, athletes,
   authors, etc.

Step 3

Compare the three epitaphs you have written. Note any similarities or differences. If you are doing this activity as a member of a class or group, compare your epitaphs with those of other classmates. What aspects of persons' lives seemed to be featured most often—their personalities, accomplishments, problems, other aspects? If you are reading this book alone, ask others to read the epitaphs you have written. Their reactions will let you consider what you have written from another person's point of view.

48

WILLIAM SHAKESPEARE, 1564-1616
(British playwright)
Good friend, for Jesus sake forbear
to dig the dust enclosed here.
Blest be the man yt pares these stones,
And cursed be he yt moves my bones.

BENJAMIN FRANKLIN, 1706-1790
(American diplomat, inventor, and printer)
The Body of
B. Franklin,
Printer;
Like the Cover of an old Book,
Its Contents torn out,
And script of its Lettering and Gilding,
Lies here, Food for Worms.
But the Work shall not be wholly lost;
For it will, as he believ'd, appear once more,
In a new & more perfect Edition,
Corrected and amended
By the Author.
He was born Jan. 6, 1706.
Died 17-

FROM ARTHUR C. HOMAN'S GRAVE IN CLEVELAND, OHIO
Once I wasn't
Then I was
Now I ain't again.

ELIZABETH CHASE AKERS, 1832-1911
(American poet)
Carve not upon a stone when I am dead
The praises which remorseful mourners give
To women's graves—a tardy recompense—
But speak them while I live.

ALEXANDER GRAHAM BELL, 1847-1922
(American inventor)
So little done, so much to do.

FROM A VERMONT CEMETERY
Here lies
the body of our Anna
Done to death
by a banana.
It wasn't the fruit
that laid her low
But the skin of the thing
that made her go.

WILLIAM BUTLER YEATS, 1865-1939
(Irish poet and playwright)
Cast a cold eye
On life, on death.
Horseman, pass by.

CLARK GABLE, 1901-1960
(American movie actor)
Back to silents!

FROM A CEMETERY IN STOWE, VERMONT
I was somebody.
Who, is no business
of yours.

FROM BOOTHILL CEMETERY IN TOMBSTONE, ARIZONA
Here lies
Lester Moore
Four slugs
From a forty-four
No Less
No More

DOROTHY PARKER, 1893-1967
(American writer, poet, and humorist)
Excuse my dust.

HARRY S TRUMAN, 1884-1972
(American President)
A good public servant.

FROM A CEMETERY IN DORSETSHIRE, ENGLAND
Here lies the body
of Margaret Bent
She kicked up her heels
And away she went

FROM A CEMETERY IN GEORGIA
I told you I was sick!

FROM A CEMETERY IN UNIONTOWN, PENNSYLVANIA
Here lies the body
of Jonathan Blake
Stepped on the gas
Instead of the brake

Periodical Bibliography

The following list of periodical articles deals with the subject matter of this chapter.

Carol Austin Bridgwater — "An Investigation of Grief," *Psychology Today*, December 1984.

Angela Engel — "It's Hard To Know How To Comfort a Friend Whose Loved One Has Died," *Glamour*, October 1983.

Daniel Goleman — "Mourning: New Studies Affirm Its Benefits," *The New York Times*, February 5, 1985.

Madge Harrh — "I've Come To Clean Your Shoes," *Reader's Digest*, December 1983.

Harold S. Kuschner — "Why Do Bad Things Happen to Good People?" *Reader's Digest*, January 1983.

Steve Laroe — "My Infant's Death: A Father's Story," *Glamour*, April 1986.

Lawrence Maloney — "A New Understanding About Death," *U.S. News & World Report*, July 11, 1983.

Monica J. Maxon — "Caring as Calling," *Christianity Today*, January 25, 1984.

Beverly McLeod — "Saying the Right Thing to the Bereaved," *Psychology Today*, December 1984.

Francine Prose — "Hers: Grief, Ordinary and Extraordinary," *The New York Times*, March 21, 1985.

Lee Ranck — "The Dying of a Friend," *engage/social action forum*, April 1986.

Paul Robinson — "Five Models for Dying," *Psychology Today*, March 1981.

Roger Rosenblatt — "Do You Feel the Deaths of Strangers?" *Time*, December 17, 1984.

Ann Kaiser Stearns — "How To Live Through Loss," *Reader's Digest*, July 1986.

U.S. News & World Report — "Coping with Grief—It Can't Be Rushed," October 26, 1983.

James Vincent — "When Laughter Is Okay at a Funeral," *Christianity Today*, August 9, 1985.

How Can Suicide Be Prevented?

♦ death and dying

"The question is not 'Should we or should we not prevent suicide?' but, rather, 'how and when should suicide be prevented?'"

Suicide Should Not Always Be Prevented

René F.W. Diekstra

Whether it is always right to stop a person from committing suicide is a significant ethical issue. The author of the following viewpoint, René F.W. Diekstra, a professor at the University of Leiden in Holland, describes his reaction to a friend's suicide. Laws concerning death are more liberal in Holland than in most other countries, and in specific, legally-defined circumstances, it is legal for a doctor in Holland to help a person commit suicide. Writing from this perspective, Diekstra concludes that his friend used good criteria for determining whether his decision to kill himself was right. In such cases, he argues, suicidal people should be allowed to make their own life-and-death decisions.

As you read, consider the following questions:

1. What are the criteria Diekstra and his colleague developed for deciding when suicide is justified? Do you agree with these criteria?
2. What, according to the author, is the crucial choice in whether to prevent suicide?

René F.W. Diekstra, "The Significance of Nico Speijer's Suicide: How and When Should Suicide Be Prevented?" *Suicide and Life-Threatening Behavior*, Spring 1986, Vol. 16, No. 1. Reprinted with permission.

On the morning of September 29, 1981, while attending a meeting of the World Health Organization on suicide, held in Athens, I was suddenly called out of the meeting room. The reason was a telephone call from the Ministry of Health in my country, The Netherlands, announcing that my mentor and friend Professor Nico Speijer had died the night before. He and his wife had put an end to their lives. Apart from my personal feelings, Nico Speijer's way of death touched profoundly upon all of us present at the meeting. Speijer was the grand old man of suicidology in the Netherlands, and, more, he was an outstanding member, even an honorary member, of the International Association for Suicide Prevention. From the birth of this organization in 1960 on, he had been an active and colorful participant in practically all of its meetings.

As can be expected in the case of a man of Speijer's status and reputation, his suicide evoked reactions nationwide. The leading newspapers and even the national TV networks made extensive mention of it. Though people's comments on the event were quite diverse, the underlying tone was generally one of understanding and sympathy. At the time of his death Speijer had been very ill with intestinal cancer and had been in great pain. His wife, herself disabled, had preferred to die with him rather than to be left behind.

Speijer's Letter

When I returned home from Athens, among the waiting mail, there was a letter written to me in the handwriting that had become so familiar over the previous 10 years. Reading the letter, knowing that he had written it just a few hours before he died, and identifying myself with what he must have felt at that moment, I felt an almost unbearable emotional pain. For the first time I fully realized what it means to be a survivor.

September 25, 1981

Dear René,

When you receive this letter, I will no longer be alive. As you know, I suffer from a carcinoma with a lot of metastases. Up to now I have been relatively capable of controlling the pain, but I cannot cope with it any longer and therefore—as you yourself will very well understand—I have decided to put an end to my life. . . .

My wife has decided to go with me. After a marriage of 40 years she prefers to die with me over having to stay behind all on her own. . . .

In the letter, further, he expressed his fear that their suicide might have a contagious influence, and he asked me to try to mitigate

54

this effect by explaining to others, especially the public, what had brought him to this decision. Speijer turned out to be perfectly right. In the 2 weeks following his death, at least four couples were known to have followed this example, as was clear from references to Speijer and his wife in the notes they left behind. Possibly there have been more since then. Why am I referring to all of this? The reason simply is that, in my opinion, the case of the Speijers is basically related to the subject of ethical issues in suicide prevention.

Respecting the Suicidal Person's Values

I am a far less committed suicide preventer than I was 15 years ago. . . . It feels to me that just as I would not want to be trapped into life, so I would not want to trap another. Just as I would not want my humanity reduced to a simple diagnostic statement, so I would not want to label anyone suicidal and respond as though this were the only significant truth about that person. As I would not want doctors deciding on the basis of their own value system what's good for me and then enforcing it, so I would not want to impose on another.

What I do feel I owe all my patients and all my friends is the benefit of my experience, knowledge and whatever caring I can offer.

Paul W. Pretzel, in *Suicide: Assessment and Intervention*, 1984.

How could it have happened that a man who had virtually all of his 76 years been a protagonist of suicide *prevention* committed suicide himself, thereby knowingly taking the risk of provoking others to do the same? A simple and definite answer would be, and some indeed have suggested this, that by the end of his life Speijer had become mentally disturbed. This, however, is gainsaid by the testimonies of those, including myself, who had been around him in the last period of his life. Surely, he was in serious pain and under great stress, due to the dreadful fact of living in a body that was rapidly becoming wrecked by a horrible disease. But mentally ill? No. Some others, wrestling with the same question, have suggested that his character played a decisive role. According to that theory, he was the kind of person who could never have passively undergone the process of dying, possibly confined to a hospital bed and dependent upon the mercy of others. Like everything else in his life, he also might have wanted to control the way, time, and place of his death. There is certainly a point here. But it only implies that people die the way they live and that for some people suicide is a more "natural" death than for others.

However, there is much more to it. A year before Speijer died, he and I had published a book whose title would probably translate into English as *Aiding Suicide: A Critical Discussion of Conditions in which Suicide Should and Should Not Be Prevented.* We had worked for almost 2 years on this text and finally came up with a set of criteria by which to decide when suicide should not necessarily be prevented and when helping with it should no longer be punishable by law. Here is a brief summary of them:

- The choice of ending life by suicide is based on a free-will decision of the person and not made under pressure by others.
- The person's condition can be described as one of unbearable physical and/or emotional pain, and improvement of this condition cannot reasonably be expected.
- The wish to die can be identified as an enduring one.
- The person, at the time of the decision to commit suicide, is *compos mentis* (i.e. not mentally disturbed).
- The suicide should be carried out in such a way that no unnecessary and preventable harm is caused to others.
- The helper should be a qualified health professional, and in case a lethal dosage of drugs is prescribed, a medical doctor should always be involved.
- The helper should never handle such cases entirely on his or her own, but should ask for professional consultation from colleagues.
- Finally, every step taken should be fully documented, and the documents should be held at the disposal of the appropriate authorities.

As it turned out, in the preparation of his death, Speijer fulfilled all these criteria. As it also turned out, no more than 3 months after his death, these criteria were officially reinforced by the court of the city of Rotterdam. A lay volunteer was convicted because she helped a woman to commit suicide in violation of the above-mentioned criteria, which were explicitly mentioned in the formulation of the sentence. It is almost certain that Speijer's suicide and the reactions of the general public to it had great influence on this sentence.

How and When To Prevent Suicide

The paradoxical thing is that from then on health professionals have been approached by a substantial number of persons asking for help with their planned suicides. Most of these requests have been rejected on the basis of the above-mentioned criteria, but, in the course of contacts with these patients, it has often been possible to provide them with other alternatives. It is my impression that a lot of them would never even have considered contacting professionals if they had not hoped to be taken seriously because of the Rotterdam case. And probably a number of unnecessary suicides have been prevented in this way.

The bottom line of this, and the significance of Speijer's suicide to me, seems to be as follows: The crucial choice is not to be or not to be, but rather how and when to be. Stated within the framework of suicide prevention, the question is not "Should we or should we not prevent suicide?" but, rather, "how and when should suicide be prevented?" Speijer's answer to the question of *when* suicide should be prevented would have been "In by far the majority of cases, but not always." His answer to the question of *how* would have been "Through a little bit of professional knowledge and training and lots of genuine human interest, or should we even say love?" In my opinion, any other answers are ethically dubious.

> *"If people clearly and unequivocally wanted to kill themselves, I would not have an ethical problem to consider. I have never seen such certainty even in people who have gone on to die by suicide."*

Suicide Should Always Be Prevented

Sam M. Heilig

Sam M. Heilig has a Masters of Social Work degree and is the executive director of the Los Angeles Suicide Prevention Center. In the following viewpoint, Heilig draws upon his personal experience as a counselor to argue that the question of whether suicide should be prevented is not really a legitimate issue. Most suicidal people do not unequivocally want to die, he argues, but rather are looking for a way to end the pain and suffering they are experiencing. The goal of suicide prevention workers is to ease the depression suicidal people feel so that death no longer seems necessary, he concludes.

As you read, consider the following questions:

1. Why does the author believe the ethics of preventing suicide should be discussed in human terms, not theoretical ones?
2. How does Heilig respond to the issue of allowing terminally ill persons to commit suicide?
3. What is the "factor of ambivalence" Heilig describes?

Sam M. Heilig, "A Personal Statement," from *Suicide: Assessment and Intervention*, Corrine Loing Hatton and Sharon McBride Valente, eds. Norwalk, CT: Appleton-Century-Crofts, 1984. Reprinted with permission.

This whole question—Is suicide prevention ethical?—has always disturbed me and left me feeling that there was something grossly inappropriate about it. My day-to-day experience simply proves to me that there are many people in the Los Angeles community, as there must be in every community, who are desperately seeking help. They come to me and they ask for help. I am not running about, trying to capture people and lock them up in hospitals. As a matter of fact, I never come into any situation calling for my services unless I am invited.

The questions about the morality of suicide prevention may possibly be prompted by an attitude, observed increasingly in our society, that we do not wish to involve ourselves in other people's troubles. The most dramatic illustration of this wish to be uninvolved with others who are in trouble is best illustrated by the cases of victim's onlookers who refuse to call police or respond to cries of a victim being murdered before their eyes on city streets.

Not a Question of Individual Freedom

Many people, of course, do not want to be engaged in the work of suicide prevention. They have every right in the world to do as they wish. However, why question the humanity of those who want to help prevent suicide? Why challenge those who need help? In my mind, such questions have always sounded specious and unreal. After 25 years of professional involvement in suicide prevention research and practice at the Los Angeles Suicide Prevention Center, I have yet to see the question of infringing the person's individual freedom during suicidal crisis emerge as a real, substantive human problem. I have been involved in helping literally thousands of individuals through a suicide episode in their lives and I cannot recall an instance where they complained or objected to my having intervened to save their life.

Of the hundreds of people I have known over the years who have worked in the field of suicide prevention, my clear impression is that they are more often than not civil libertarians who would defend individual rights and freedom. It is possible, of course, to conduct a discussion on theoretical terms, but, personally, I find it very difficult to confront the issue in other than human terms. The basis of my opposition rests on two obvious realities: (1) The more important is the fact that the suicidal person is rarely if ever concerned with individual freedom, but rather desperately searching for some means of relieving personal anguish and suffering; (2) I know full well that despite our best efforts, even in those instances where the would-be suicide is incarcerated they are free to end their life if determined to do so.

"OH, LEAVE HIM ALONE. HE'S ONLY DOING HIS THING."

Any discussion of the ethics of suicide prevention usually raises the question: What shall we do about the person with a terminal illness, suffering unbearable pain in the last few weeks of life? Most well-meaning reasonable people would probably agree that there are serious reservations about unnecessarily extending the life of a dying person for a short period when that means enduring so much more dreadful physical pain and suffering. Very often medical caregivers may echo the dying patient's articulate questions about the purpose of extending or prolonging life. Most humane and reasonable people would agree that a person who wished to die and put an end to suffering should be allowed to do so.

This is really not a question of suicide prevention but rather one of allowing people to die with dignity. The difference here is that the person is in the process of dying and none of us is going to prevent that death. This is a situation very different from that, let us say, of a 25-year-old woman, who wants to end her life because she is temporarily distraught in response to the loss of a lover. When people are in the terminal phase of an illness, the question usually revolves around what medical intervention we should provide in an effort to extend life. Frequently, in a terminal illness, it is not a matter of preventing suicide, but rather one of allowing death to come. As it so happens, many people who have been leaders in the field of suicide prevention have also engaged in the study and the work involved in understanding the dying process, with the objective of helping people to die more comfortably.

Ambivalence

Everyone who has worked with people who are suicidal and has tried to understand something about that particularly poignant paradox has commented on the factor of ambivalence. . . . I repeat that we have all observed that suicidal people are pulled in contrary directions, wishing to die and to live at the same time. This ambivalence is really what plagues me and what answers the first question, for if people clearly and unequivocally wanted to kill themselves, I would not have an ethical problem to consider. I have never seen such certainty even in people who have gone on to die by suicide. . . .

What one observes with people who are suicidal is that the problem is not one of individual freedom—whether a person has the right to dispose of his life as he wishes—but rather how to reduce the suffering of that person. People who are suicidal are obviously in a state of physical or psychic pain and anguish. It is really the task of suicide prevention to relieve it. When people exhaust their own capacities to reduce their suffering and see no hope that their situation will ever improve, many will arrive at the idea of suicide as a way out. It is not really death which is wanted but rather an end to suffering and pain. One has only to spend a day in any suicide prevention center or talk to any suicidal person and this becomes eminently clear.

I know that I, personally, am unable to prevent suicide, but I can certainly help people who are suicidal to find other ways out of their problems when they seek my help. I am currently working with a woman who is chronically and severely depressed, who always has the idea of suicide in her mind. She keeps a lethal dose of pills on hand in case she should decide to kill herself. Some years ago, she made a serious suicidal attempt with pills and was saved by prompt medical intervention. She has not made a suicide attempt in more than 5 years. She and I both know that I am unable to prevent her suicide should she decide to take the pills in her possession. She knows she can do this any time and I know that, too.

I have a question to ask those who think that to prevent a person's suicide might be an infringement of personal liberty: Why does this woman continue to come to me? She and I both hope that her depression will pass or that we will find a way to relieve it. We both know that in many people, depressions simply go away, and we also know that frequently, with a proper medication, the intensity of depressed feelings can be considerably reduced. . . .

More Should Be Done To Prevent Suicide

Then, there is an overwhelming reality to consider: the past 25 years of the development of suicide prevention programs in this country. Why have suicide prevention programs been initiated during this period in more than 200 cities throughout the United States? And what about the tens of thousands of people who come to these suicide prevention centers asking for help? This may be the real ethical question in the area of suicide prevention: Are we providing sufficient resources to assist these thousands of people who are so desperate and whose lives are in such danger? Those of us who work daily in suicide prevention know the terrible straits and the dreadful suffering of the people who ask us for help. We also know our own inadequacies, our insufficient resources and our many other weaknesses. And finally we know that because of our inadequacies many of these people who are seeking our help will go on to commit suicide, in spite of all our efforts.

"Silence on the subject of suicide contributes to the perpetuation of the stigma and . . . may prevent young people from getting help."

Suicide Education Can Reduce Teen Suicide

Charlotte P. Ross

The following viewpoint is an excerpt from a teen suicide prevention program developed for schools by Charlotte P. Ross, the Executive Director of the Suicide Prevention and Crisis Center of San Mateo County in California. Ross believes that many students face the problem of suicide either because they are suicidal or because a friend who is suicidal comes to them for help. She concludes that education can eliminate the secrecy surrounding suicide, correct the distorted images many people have of suicide, and help students find out where they can go for help.

As you read, consider the following questions:

1. What role does denial play in preventing discussion of suicide, according to the author?
2. What are the danger signs the author lists that indicate someone may be considering suicide?
3. What four things does the author recommend the friend of a suicidal person keep in mind?

Charlotte P. Ross, from the California Youth Suicide Prevention School Program, Teacher's Guide, 1985. Reprinted with permission.

Teenage suicide has risen dramatically in recent years so that it is now the second leading cause of death among young people 15-24. Only accidents—many of which may actually be suicides—are a more common form of death among teenagers. It is highly likely, therefore, that your school may have experienced the suicide of a student or an attempted suicide. It is also highly likely that some of the students in your classes are struggling with feelings of sadness and depression that could lead them to consider suicide as a possible means of coping with their problems.

And—just as you may have to cope with depressed students in your class—your students may also be asked to assist a friend who confides that he or she is considering suicide. Research studies show that teenagers overwhelmingly turn to their peers in such a time of crisis. Unfortunately, many teenagers are ill-equipped to help a friend in trouble and may even—out of ignorance or fear—enter into pacts of secrecy with a friend who is depressed and fail to seek help for fear of betraying that friendship.

Goals of the Curriculum

It is the prevalence of suicide among teenagers and the characteristic patterns of teenage rescuing that provide the impetus for this curriculum. In seeking to prevent suicide among youth, this program has dual goals. First is to help students better understand suicidal feelings and how to deal with them so that they are not overwhelmed and bewildered. Second is to enhance students' skills in helping others who are feeling suicidal by teaching them (1) how to respond appropriately to a friend and (2) how to identify and use the resources available in the community to help a peer who is feeling depressed.

Underlying both these goals is the intention to create an atmosphere in which students can speak appropriately about suicide with each other and with adults. Suicide is a topic wrapped in a shroud of silence, fear, stigma and half-truths. By bringing it out in the open for thoughtful examination, suicide and the feelings which lead up to it can be better understood by young people. . . .

Dealing with Our Own Fears

There are a number of reasons we fear talking about suicide. One reason is our own *ambivalence* and anxiety about voluntary death of a young person. All the projections, defenses and rejections that operate in relation to adolescence on the one hand, and to death in general and voluntary death in particular, on the other, converge in the suicidal adolescent. It is not uncommon for adults to react to a teenage suicide in ways nearly as contrary and irrational as the act itself, responding both with compassion and anger.

Another powerful reason for avoiding talk about suicide is *denial*. If we feel we're at fault or to blame for a suicide in some way, we may react by denying that it actually happened. If we believe we've failed, it would be tremendously distressing to talk about the suicide. And the idea of adolescent suicide is in itself so difficult to comprehend that we may even deny its existence because it makes no sense to us.

However, young people are not denying that it exists. They know about suicide, and they talk about it. They see it in the newspapers, hear it in popular music, read about it in their favorite novels or in their assigned reading. Unfortunately, much of what they hear is distorted or only half-truths. One of the most common indirect messages young people receive about suicide is that talking about depression or suicide is not appropriate. Yet silence on the subject of suicide contributes to the perpetuation of the stigma and secrecy that surround this topic, and conveys clearly that it's a topic adults are not comfortable discussing. This may prevent young people from getting help.

Dangerous Myths

When youngsters who want to learn about suicide are not provided with reliable information, they often seek out what they can as best they can. Often, their sources are rumor and speculation, and their experts are other teenagers. With a subject as fraught with dangerous myths, half-truths, and misconceptions as suicide, the results of inquiry can be tragic. For example, the belief that suicidal impulses indicate self-pity, inadequacy, or "insanity" may further damage a youth's already fragile self-esteem and add a secondary panic reaction to an existing depression. . . .

A suicidal youth . . . may not wait for life to teach him that his feelings are normal and understandable, or that there are ways of dealing with them. It is my contention that if he is to learn this in time, a part of his education must be directed toward that goal.

Charlotte P. Ross, in *Youth Suicide*, 1985.

Another form of denial by adults is not believing that young people experience feelings of sadness and depression profound enough to warrant suicide. Since these are the "best years of their lives," their problems cannot be serious enough to be taken seriously. However, each person's view of the world is different and youngsters take their hurts, disappointments and losses as seriously as do adults. The evidence clearly suggests that suicide is not *confined* to any one age, economic, geographical, or social group. Nor is it *absent* from any group.

Often, we fear that if we talk about teenage suicide, we will make it happen by putting ideas into the heads of impressionable youngsters or opening up feelings that they can't deal with. In truth, the evidence suggests overwhelmingly that *not* talking about suicide creates barriers for young people who are trying to understand what they are feeling. Further, talking about feelings in a caring, warm and direct way with a youngster who is depressed can be the single most effective means of suicide prevention. Compassion for suicidal feelings does not mean condoning the suicidal act.

Another fear of teachers is that it is inappropriate to burden all your students with the topic of youth suicide when only a small proportion of them may take any suicidal action. Surveys indicate, however, that about 10 percent of high school students report that they have made at least one suicide attempt, and 40 percent of them have thought about suicide to the point of deciding how to do it. Three-quarters of high school students report they have had a friend turn to them for help. Young people need to learn how to respond effectively to the confidences of their friends, and they need to learn to understand their own feelings.

Youngsters get depressed and often don't even know what they feel has a name, much less that others sometimes feel as they do and that help can be found. When we're depressed, we all need someone to listen to us, regardless of how old we are. There's a saying that sums it up well: "A problem shared is a problem halved."

Unfortunately, being open isn't always enough. Although many adolescents resist the notion of professional help, that help is needed when something as serious as suicide is considered. Students and teachers need to know where help is available, and how to get it and use it effectively. Many communities have suicide prevention, crisis centers or hotlines. In addition, all communities have local mental health programs to provide professional help when needed. . . .

One of the goals of this program is to create an atmosphere in which students can speak comfortably about suicide with each other and with adults, so that they explore questions of feelings, trust and confidentiality that will enable them to recognize their own feelings of depression and to function as effective helpers to one another. . . .

The Signals Suicidal Teenagers Send

Young people who are thinking about suicide often give signals in advance of what they are contemplating. The key lies in our ability to recognize and respond to this cry for help.

Teenagers who are coping with depression are likely to engage in patterns of behavior that are somewhat different from adults.

There are two basic patterns of behavior that emerge for coping with their depression before turning to suicide as a final solution to their problems. The most common pattern displays passive behavior: gloominess, non-communication, withdrawal and isolation. Another pattern is that of aggressive behavior: disobedience, sarcasm, defiance and rebelliousness. . . .

There are a number of specific danger or warning signs that someone may be suicidal:

1. *Suicide Threats*. Some people believe that anyone who talks about suicide won't really do it. However, before committing suicide, most young people give clues to their suicidal thoughts. They may make direct statements about their intention to end their lives, or less direct comments that they might as well be dead or that their friends and family would be better off without them. Even though it's difficult to imagine someone you know could be thinking of such an action, suicide threats and similar statements should always be taken seriously. They are a very real sign of danger.

Life-Saving Education

The ultimate prevention of suicide lies in public education specifically about the clues to suicide. Most people would agree that the best prevention is primary prevention; here, perhaps more than anywhere else, an ounce of prevention can be priceless, life-saving. The primary prevention of suicide lies in education. The route is through teaching one another and that large, amorphous group known as the public, that suicide can happen to anyone, that there are verbal and behavioral clues that can be looked for (if one but has the threshold to see and hear them when they occur), and that help is available.

Edwin Shneidman, *Definition of Suicide*, 1985.

---

2. *Previous Attempts*. People who have tried to kill themselves before, even if their attempts didn't seem very serious, are also at risk if they didn't get help to resolve the issues troubling them. Unless they are helped, they may try again.

3. *Sudden Changes in Behavior or Personality*. The shy person who suddenly becomes a thrill-seeker or the outgoing person who becomes withdrawn, unfriendly and disinterested may be giving off signals that something is seriously wrong. Other differences include changes in sleeping patterns, lack of interest or sudden kindness to friends and family; loss of appetite; loss of weight; neglect of school work; lack of interest in personal appearance; long periods of solitude, etc.

4. *Recent loss, hurt or humiliation*. Death of family member or friend or "getting in trouble."

5. *Final Arrangements.* Giving away prized personal belongings, such as a record collection, is a particularly serious sign. In effect, the young person is making his or her will, attempting to get personal affairs in order.

Since almost all teens engage in rapid mood swings and experiment with aggressive or passive behavior during adolescence in response to the many changes they are experiencing, it is sometimes difficult to differentiate between normal adolescent behaviors and those that indicate something is seriously wrong. Most of these signs can be considered part of normal growth unless 1) they persist over a long time; and 2) several are evidenced at once. . . .

Students Turn to Friends for Help

Several studies have asked high school students whom they would tell if they should ever consider suicide. One study, for example, offered the following choices: parent, other adult, teacher, school counselor, school nurse, doctor, friend, minister or "other." "Friend" was selected as first choice in 91 percent of the responses.

This tendency to turn to peers in crisis appears to reflect the adolescent struggle with dependency that is characteristic of this age. Adults are often viewed apprehensively, more likely to interfere than to understand. In contrast, peers are perceived as more likely to empathize, less likely to interfere, and more likely to keep a secret.

However, some of these very same qualities that make friends the confidants of choice also make them dangerously inadequate as counselors and rescuers. Adolescents' willingness to keep a confidence, their disinclination—or inability—to actively intervene, and their lack of knowledge regarding what could or should be done, often makes them silent partners in a youth suicide. . . .

The friend to whom the young person contemplating suicide turns has four things to keep in mind: 1) to *listen* to the other person; 2) to *be honest* about their feelings in response; 3) to *share feelings* with the other person, so that he or she no longer feels alone; and 4) to *get help* from an adult who can support the young person to get professional counseling. This latter point is especially critical. Students should be reminded that keeping a secret may mean losing a friend. But sharing a secret can save a friend.

"Discussions and increased awareness of suicide may actually put the idea of it into children's minds."

Suicide Education May Increase Teen Suicide

William Smith and Howard Hurwitz

Those who oppose suicide education programs in schools often argue that schools cannot effectively deal with social problems. In Part I of the following viewpoint, William Smith contends that the government should not support school suicide programs because those programs may in fact make teen suicide a more serious problem. Smith is a research assistant at the Heritage Foundation, a conservative think tank. Dr. Howard Hurwitz in Part II writes that schools do not handle social problems well and thus should leave suicide prevention up to counselors and parents. Hurwitz is a regular columnist for *The Union Leader*, a daily newspaper in Manchester, New Hampshire.

As you read, consider the following questions:

1. What school programs designed to cure social ills does Smith criticize?
2. List two objections Smith has to current youth suicide programs.
3. What does Hurwitz suggest parents do to prevent teen suicide?

William Smith, "The Youth Suicide Problem: Washington Could Make It Worse," *Heritage Foundation Executive Memorandum*, September 17, 1986. Reprinted with permission.
Howard Hurwitz, "Should Suicide Prevention Be High School Course?" *The Union Leader*, January 30, 1985. Reprinted with the author's permission.

I

It generally is now accepted that educators must return to basics. Yet this has not stopped the proliferation of school programs designed to cure social ills, not to educate. "Education" programs aim at solving the problems of nuclear war, drunk driving, drug abuse, sex discrimination, child abuse, and global conflict. Some programs have more merit than others. One that, it seems, clearly would not attempts to address the distressing problem of youth suicide.

On July 14, [1986] the House passed by voice vote the Youth Suicide Prevention Act (H.R. 4650). The bill would provide $1 million to fund a grant program in the Department of Education to assist local educational agencies and private nonprofit organizations to establish and operate programs of youth suicide prevention.

Good Intentions, Bad Programs

It is hard to fault the good intentions of the legislation. If a tried and tested method of preventing youth suicides existed, few Americans would oppose making it widely available. Such a method does not exist, and H.R. 4650 is not going to find one. What H.R. 4650 is likely to yield are programs run by unlicensed psychologists or other nonprofessionals and programs whose content will be kept secret from parents. It is even possible that H.R. 4650 could weaken the traditional and justifiable social stigma attached to suicide. The net result could exacerbate the problem.

Similar legislation in the Senate (S. 2551) would create a "National Center on Youth Suicide" within the Department of Health and Human Services. The Center would oversee a national public awareness campaign and create a national resource center to disseminate technical assistance, information, and organizational help to those wishing to help prevent youth suicide. By concentrating resources on research, this Senate bill recognizes better than the House bill that there is no clear answer to youth suicide that can be handled by legislative action. Yet S. 2251 still has a serious flaw—it would fund programs and raise public awareness without giving any reliable guides for action.

Increased Awareness Is Dangerous

Much of this congressional legislation is based on the assumption that increased awareness and discussion of suicide is the means of its prevention. Yet evidence suggests the opposite. Discussions and increased awareness of suicide may actually put the idea of it into children's minds. Suicides generally increase,

70

for example, after television news or drama that centers on suicide. One youth suicide in a neighborhood or school sometimes triggers others. Cautions Dr. David Shaffer, Chief of Psychiatry at Columbia University's New York State Psychiatric Institute: discussions of suicide "can lower the threshold of vulnerable kids." Adds Dr. Harold M. Voth, Chief of Staff at the Veterans Administration Medical Center in Topeka, Kansas: Emotionally charged "rap sessions" run by nonprofessionals . . . may actually be one of the factors that leads to some suicides. Another danger of the proposed legislation is that funding might go to controversial programs that actually look benignly upon the act of youth suicide. There are even those who feel that children should be informed of their "right" to commit suicide. Others dwell morbidly on the topics of death and dying or argue that suicide should be held out as an option to those in physical or mental distress.

Morbid and Morose

[Schools] add to the teen suicide epidemic . . . through "death education" classes, and through textbooks and classes that dwell on nuclear war and environmental destruction.

Many students are also subjected to classes that morbidly focus on death and dying. "Few schools do not plague children with death education," said education writer Barbara M. Morris in her book, *Change Agents in the Schools*. "It can be taught as an identifiable course, or, more often, woven into existing subjects from kindergarten through grade twelve." Besides morose reading assignments and incessant discussions and questionnaires that probe the students' attitudes concerning death, students may be taken on "field trips" to mortuaries, cemeteries, and crematoria. . . . Suicide is the natural fallout of these classes.

William F. Jasper, *The New American*, July 28, 1986.

Congress thus should consider warily any legislation funding suicide prevention programs. Federal efforts, moreover, should be run from the Justice Department to make it clear that suicide violates the law. Legislation should impose legal sanctions on any program that passively or actively encourages youths to commit suicide. Legislation also should ensure that any programs are in keeping with the Hatch Amendment, which requires that students cannot be subject to psychological testing without their parents' permission.

If there is to be a role for the Department of Education, it should be to use existing research resources to discover how curriculum may allay the suicide problem. Adolescence is a time when a child learns that life entails pains as well as joys. As such, a curriculum that emphasized "overcoming difficulties" might be far more effective in discouraging suicide that any well-meaning "awareness" program. Education Secretary William Bennett points out that a good curriculum can help build good and balanced character.

Untested Programs

With a problem as delicate as youth suicide lawmakers should not rush to legislate just to show they are "doing something." Action based on insufficient knowledge can be worse than no action at all. Until the mental health community itself has reached a consensus about the best method of prevention; until reliable and accurate statistics on the problem are compiled; and until parents can be assured that school programs will not encourage suicide, lawmakers should stick to encouraging research. Congress is playing a dangerous game when it seeks to fund untested programs that experiment with children in matters of life and death.

II

At an end-of-year convention in Dallas [in 1984], psychiatrists proposed that high schools introduce suicide prevention programs. The psychiatrists must be nuts to think that high schools struggling with functional illiteracy can be a force for sanity in an increasingly deranged society.

Teenage suicides have climbed to "epidemic proportions," panelists proclaimed. The National Center for Health Statistics estimates that more than 6,000 people 15 to 24 years of age killed themselves in 1983.

That is more than five times the number who committed suicide in 1950. I would not stake my life on the accuracy of the statistics. Too many variables enter into the circumstances surrounding a death, although the immediate cause may be clear to coroners.

The alarm was sounded by psychiatrists joined by Lt. Gov. Alfred DelBello of New York, who resigned as of Feb. 1, [1985] to seek greener pastures in the private sector.

Part of DelBello's busy work as second in command with little to do in New York was service as co-chairman of the National Committee on Youth Suicide Prevention. In Dallas, he called for a Congressional commission to study the causes of adolescent suicides. We need such a commission like we need the proverbial hole in the head. Congress will be wise to leave suicide to the alleged experts in the private sector where the American Association of Suicidology is working fulltime.

Parents Can Prevent Suicide

Suicide can be prevented. Apart from the great majority of attempts that are unsuccessful, there are approaches that might have worked, if . . . The "if" factor is probably explored more fully by parents than any other group. One "if" that can be invoked quickly is the removal of guns from the home. Most teenagers who kill themselves do so with firearms.

I am no advocate of gun control. Parents must, however, weigh the necessity of arms around the house with their availability to youngsters who show the remotest signs of instability.

Better than arms around the house are parents at home. Typical American fathers spend "an average of 37 seconds a day with their infant children," according to some statisticians. "American parents," we are informed, "spend less time with their children than any other nation of the world."

It might be argued that parents contribute to teenage suicide and the rate would drop if parents were out. These are the parents who drink to excess, smoke pot and use harder stuff with little effort to conceal their drug dependence from children.

The Media's Role

Suicide statistics are cold, but the media can be counted upon to enliven the dull with the macabre. There is sure to be a mound of studies showing the relationship between escalating teenage suicides and media saturation. The proof can never be conclusive, because social science does not lend itself to exact measurement. Even if the belief were widespread that publicity adds to the suicide rate, there is the little matter of freedom of the press.

Suicide centers are springing up. The head of one such center in Los Angeles advises us that adolescent suicide is aimed at "the cessation of intolerable emotion, unendurable pain." Agreed. Where do we go from here?

Schools Cannot Solve Social Problems

There are multiple causes for teenage suicide and multiple ways of heading youths off before the point of no return. One way is the one-on-one counseling by parent or wiser head. A way that is furthest from common sense is an anti-suicide course in high school. I foresee such an approach as on par with drug prevention programs, a part of every high school health education curriculum for four decades.

The track record of schools in preventing social abuses is so rotten as to prohibit meddling in highly personal life or death decisions.

"Suicide . . . is the third-biggest killer of young people."

Teen Suicide Is a Growing Problem

Mary Giffin and Carol Felsenthal

The rate of teen suicide has been steadily increasing, according to Mary Giffin and Carol Felsenthal, the authors of the following viewpoint. They cite several studies which show that in addition to the official statistics on completed suicides, millions of teenagers have considered suicide and have attempted suicide. Most teenagers do not actually want to die, Giffin and Felsenthal state, and many suicides can be prevented if parents take action when their teenagers show signs of being suicidal. Giffin is a psychiatrist and the director of the Irene Jocelyn Clinic of the North Shore Mental Health Association in Illinois. Felsenthal is a syndicated columnist and author.

As you read, consider the following questions:

1. For what reasons do the authors believe the rate of teen suicide is even higher than the statistics suggest?
2. Why do Giffin and Felsenthal think that even young children between the ages of 5 and 14 can be suicidal?
3. What facts do the authors cite to prove their argument that teen suicide is preventable?

Every day, an average of 18 young Americans kill themselves—6,500 every year. Every *hour*, 57 children and adolescents in the United States attempt to destroy themselves—well over 1,000 attempts every day.

Obviously, young people, who we like to believe have everything to look forward to, do not share our optimistic view of their futures. At the Chicago-Read Mental Health Center, 300 of the 475 suicides committed by Read patients in 1976 were young people. At a Chicago-area suicide hotline, the phone rings every twenty seconds. Dr. Michael Peck, one of the country's leading suicidologists, estimates that each year in the United States "somewhere in the neighborhood of a million or more children move in and out of suicidal crises. . . ."

In researching their book *Teenage Rebellion*, Rev. Truman E. Dollar and psychiatrist Grace H. Ketterman surveyed 100 teens. Thirty-four percent answered yes to the question, "Have you ever seriously considered suicide?" Thirty-two percent said yes to, "Did you make specific plans to take your life?" When the authors asked, "Have you actually attempted suicide?" a whopping 14 percent said yes.

In a recent study of 7,000 high school students, one of every five reported severe problems with self-esteem, feelings of failure, alienation, loneliness, lack of self-confidence, low self-regard, and thoughts of suicide. Three Chicago researchers who surveyed 1,385 teens in the late 1970s and in 1980 found 20 percent feeling emotionally empty, confused most of the time, and that they would rather die than go on living.

Many more young people die of suicide than of cancer. Every year the death rate for childhood cancers falls (43 percent since 1950) and the suicide rate rises (a shocking 300 percent in the last two decades).

Suicides Are Underreported

Today, only accidents and homicides claim more young lives than suicide. And anyone with even a passing knowledge of the subject agrees that a great many of the deaths that go down in the records as accidents or homicides are really suicides. As the late Dr. Gregory Zilboorg, psychiatrist-in-chief of the United Nations, put it, "Statistical data on suicides as compiled today deserves little credence. All too many suicides are not reported as such." The number of suicides is, *at the very least*, twice what is reported.

For, even in these nearly tabooless times, there are few more grotesque skeletons in the family closet than that of a son or daughter who has committed suicide. It is the most personal, the most terrible of rebukes, and parents will go to outrageous lengths to hide it. Dr. Dominick DiMaio, former Medical Examiner for New York City, explained, "Families sometimes will tell you all kinds of stories to make a suicide look like an accident. A kid blows his brains out with a gun, or jumps off a building. The parents come in and tell us he was playing Russian roulette, or that he slipped while playing on the roof." . . .

Unsettling Figures

Suicide is a personal concern of most high school students and a serious concern of 1 out of 4 of these students. From 1 out of 8 to 1 out of 12 high school students have actually made an attempt. That such unsettling figures are not gross overestimates of the problem is indicated by the convergence of several other studies. It has become clear that if we wish to be of help to troubled adolescents, we need not target our efforts solely at the seriously suicidal young persons; it seems that most high school students may need our attention.

Kim Smith and Sylvia Crawford, *Suicide & Life-Threatening Behavior*, Fall 1986.

It is not only the shame attached to suicide that keeps the real numbers so inaccurately low. Officials at the National Center for Health Statistics do not record a death as suicide unless there is proof that suicide was intentional; that it was a case of premeditated self-destruction. A suicide note is normally required, but only 15 percent of suicides leave notes. Thus, in the absence of a note, the person who drinks Drano, "falls" out a window, or shoots himself in the head while "cleaning" a gun will probably be omitted from the statistics.

Suicide: The Number One Killer

Suicide, the statisticians remind us, is the third-biggest killer of young people, *behind* accidents and homicides. Many of us believe that suicide is really the number one killer; that many of the homicide and accident victims are really suicides in disguise. For example, a recent study in Philadelphia revealed that more than 25 percent of murder victims cause their own deaths by picking a fight with someone who had a weapon. In one case, a teenager, who knew his gun was unloaded, brandished it at police officers, inciting them to shoot him in self defense. . . .

Auto fatalities, which, in any given year, account for about 37 percent of all deaths in the 15-24-year-old group, probably represent the biggest block of suicides disguised as accidents. The person killed in a head-on collision, while driving at night in a car with no headlights on the wrong side of an expressway, would probably be pronounced an accident victim—unless there was positive proof of suicide.

Forensic experts speculate that approximately one quarter of these "accidents" are deliberate. Adding these so-called "autocides" to suicides, they argue, easily makes suicide the number one killer. . . .

We think that many so-called "accidental" poisonings are also actually suicide attempts. Each year brings one hundred thousand cases of intentional self-poisonings among children ages five to fourteen. Dr. Matilda McIntire and Dr. Caro Angle compared fifty young poisoning victims with fifty other children of similar age and background. They found that 88 percent of the poisoning victims, compared to only 12 percent of the controls, had a history of behavior problems. These children were also more likely to have had alcoholic, hostile, or rejecting parents. . . .

Suicide Among Young Children

When Pittsburgh psychologist Maria Kovacs surveyed 127 elementary school children, 41 percent admitted having thought about suicide. Michael Peck's research suggests that "up to 10 percent of the youngsters in any public school classroom may be considered at some risk for suicide."

Although there are no reliable figures for those under ten, there are figures for 10-14-year-olds. Rates for that group have risen nearly as fast as the rate for 15-24-year-olds. In the decade between 1968 and 1978 the rate increased by 32 percent.

We know now that depression, the most common impetus to suicide, also strikes children. Depression is not, as we might like to think, the exclusive property of the middle-aged and elderly. . . .

Suicide Among College Students

In 1976, half the deaths on a large midwestern campus were due to suicide—a figure that remains constant nationally. A few years ago, a researcher studying a random sample of 792 college students, of all grade levels, found that 30 percent had entertained suicidal thoughts during an academic year. Freshman year—the first time away from home—is, not surprisingly, the toughest. According to psychiatrist Lee Robbins Gardner of Columbia University's College of Physicians and Surgeons, one study of college freshmen revealed that 70 percent had thought of suicide in one given year. While writing *Too Young to Die*, a book about youth and suicide first published in 1976, Francine Klagsbrun sent questionnaires to a randomly selected group of high school and college students. More than one in ten said that they had actually attempted suicide. . . .

As high as the suicide death rate is, it seems moderate when compared to the attempt rate. For every young person who completes suicide, there may be fifty to one hundred others who attempt it and "fail." . . . At the very least, every hour fifty-seven American children and teens attempt suicide. The incidence of suicide attempts has increased by as much as 3,000 percent per year.

Suicide Is Preventable

The fact that the attempt rate so outstrips the completed rate offers us hope. . . . Most young people who attempt suicide do not want to die. Suicide is, in fact, the nation's number one *preventable* health problem—preventable because experts believe that, except for a very few, all the people who commit suicide want to live.

They die because they believe they are not loved. And so parents can prevent their children from becoming just another grim statistic. As Dr. E.S. Shneidman of the UCLA School of Medicine put it, "Until the very moment that the bullet or barbiturate finally snuffs out life's last breath, the suicidal person wants desperately to live. He is begging to be saved." Dr. M.S. Weiss of the University of Missouri Medical Center recently completed a study showing that many young people who attempt suicide have a "relatively low psychological intent" to go through with it. They may be trying to force their parents to pay attention to them or they may be trying to punish their parents. They are performing a desperate version of holding their breath until turning blue. . . .

Teenagers Want To Be Saved

Nobody commits suicide out of the blue. People, especially young people, give warnings repeatedly, as if to plead, "Please help me. I beg you. Please help me. I don't really want to die." Study after study has shown that approximately 80 percent of people who committed suicide gave repeated warnings. . . .

Nine out of ten teenage suicide attempts take place in the home. Seventy percent of teens who attempt suicide do so . . . when their parents are home. And they do so between the hours of three in the afternoon and midnight, when they can be seen, stopped, and saved. If they really wanted to die they would not take the chance of being discovered. (Adults choose the hours between midnight and dawn to kill themselves.)

Another hopeful statistic is that in the few months before committing suicide, 75 percent of victims had visited their family doctors. Many also were seeing a psychiatrist—other forms of cries for help which, in this country at this time, most often go unheeded.

For it is one of the most pervasive myths of suicide that once a child decides to commit suicide, there's nothing we can do to prevent it. There is plenty we can do. We can, in almost all cases, save our children's lives.

"The facts behind youth suicide suggest that we do not face a growing problem in the 1980s."

Teen Suicide Is Not a Growing Problem

Allan C. Carlson and Andy Hilger

Allan C. Carlson is the editor of *Persuasion at Work,* a conservative newsletter published by the Rockford Institute. Andy Hilger is a journalist and the president of radio station WJON in St. Cloud, Minnesota. In the following viewpoint, Carlson and Hilger argue that teen suicide is not as serious a problem as many people believe. In Part I Carlson examines the statistics on teen suicide and concludes that suicide is not a crisis in American society. Hilger argues in Part II that many professionals exaggerate the suicide rate and do not realize that religion and stronger families are the most effective ways to prevent teen suicide.

As you read, consider the following questions:

1. What statistics do both Carlson and Hilger cite to prove that teen suicide is not a crisis?
2. Carlson argues that "a whole industry" has developed from the youth suicide issue. What does he think is wrong with this industry?
3. What is wrong with the way the suicide prevention movement views parents, according to Hilger?

Allan C. Carlson, "Coping with Teen Suicides," *The Washington Times,* July 11, 1986. Reprinted with the author's permission.
Andy Hilger, "Suicide," *Human Life Issues,* Summer 1986. Reprinted with the permission of the author who wishes to credit Allan Carlson of the Rockford Institute whose research was necessary for this article.

I

There are few greater tragedies than a youth's taking his own life. Between 1955 and 1975, the number of such suicides in the United States rose 300 percent. Every year now about 5,000 Americans between the ages of 15 and 24 kill themselves.

Yet heavy media attention has only recently focused on the problem. Feature stories by the major news magazines and several made-for-TV movies, including CBS's *Silence of the Heart*, have dramatized the adolescent suicide theme. Several bills are pending before Congress that would create a national teen-suicide-prevention program.

Before rushing its creation, though, it seems appropriate to step back for a moment and assess what we already know about youth suicide. Do we actually face a crisis? What are the causes? Who stands behind this call for expansion of the welfare state?

The Statistics

Addressing the first question, the facts behind youth suicide suggest that we do not face a growing problem in the 1980s. It is true that the 1960s and early 1970s witnessed a dramatic increase in the number of youth suicides. Yet even in 1975—the peak year for teen suicides—the total number among 10- to 14-year-olds in a nation of 220 million people was 170. Among 15- to 19-year-olds, it was 1,594. Since 1975, moreover, the numbers have stabilized.

Viewed internationally, the American problem is not a crisis. Among young males, the U.S. suicide rate of 19.7 per 100,000 teenagers is below the rates found in Switzerland (33.5), Germany (21.2), and Norway (20.2). For young women, the American rate (4.6) falls below that found in Denmark (5.0), France (5.0), and Japan (6.4).

Professionals have failed, moreover, to develop a theory that would justify government intervention. According to Charlotte Ross, director of the San Mateo (Calif.) County Suicide Prevention and Crisis Center, today's teen-agers go through the normal agonies of adolescence while their world is being shaken by "social tremors" such as divorce, working mothers, remarriage, and "reconstituted families." Yet on other occasions, the same analysts go out of their way to deny that divorce or working mothers are to blame.

Lurking behind such disjointed logic are ambitious professionals who sense new government money just over the horizon. Social workers want funding for expanded "home visitation" to investigate the character of parents. Psychologists note that "there is always the need for more and better counseling services."

Indeed, a whole industry has arisen in the last decade to face the youth suicide crisis, including the American Association of Suicidology, National Committee on Youth Suicide Prevention, and the Youth Suicide National Center.

Honest research on the problem, though, points to different solutions. Instead of endorsing growth of the "therapeutic state," this research highlights the continued importance of religion and traditional family life as a protection against suicide. For example, one recent study shows what common sense suggests: the highest suicide rates are found among families with unmarried or divorced parents; the lowest rates are found among intact nuclear families.

Using data for the United States between 1954 and 1978, sociologist Stephen Stack has shown that indicators of spreading

Trends in the Youth Suicide Rate And Other Variables

Suicides of 15-24 year-olds per 100,000 persons

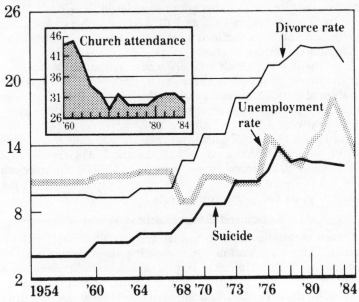

Only youth unemployment figures available

"domestic individualism" (divorce and mothers' participation in the labor force) and religious individualism (absence from church) are both highly related to the rise in the youth suicide rate. Mr. Stack has also calculated that a 1 percent increase in youth church attendance would produce a 1.4 percent *decrease* in youth suicide.

The Need for Religion and Family

From this perspective, religion and the family are not mere options for us; they are necessary if lives are to be saved.

This does not mean we can call on governments to restore vigorous religions and strong families. Such acts cannot be performed by the state. . . .

The more important tasks must be addressed outside Washington. For those religious groups which succumbed in recent decades to the allure of political activism and to theologies shaped by ideological fads, there is need to return to their spiritual roots. As modern social research shows, stronger families would follow, and the youth suicide rate would decline.

II

It is amazing the amount of media attention that suicide is getting today. Especially suicide among the young. To be sure, there are few tragedies more shattering than a youth taking his own life. Yet, despite the fact that youth suicides in the United States rose by 300% between 1955 and 1975, the numbers have since leveled off and even declined a bit. Yet, the media coverage and professional interest increases. . . .

It is true that the 1960s and 1970s saw a dramatic increase in the number of youth suicides. But, in the peak year of 1975, within a nation of over 200 million persons, the total number of suicides among 5-9 year olds was zero; among 10-14 year olds 170; among 15-19 year olds 1,594; and among 20-24 year olds 3,142. When viewed globally, the U.S. suicide rate per 100,000 male adolescents is 19.7. Switzerland has a rate of 33.5, Austria 33.6, Germany 21.2 and Norway 20.2. Among young women per 100,000 the American rate is 4.6, Denmark is 5.0, France 5.0 and Japan 6.4. Over the past ten years the youth suicide rate is receding. . . .

Expanded Governmental Power

Governments have begun to turn the so-called youth suicide "crisis" into an occasion for expanding their power. . . . The United States Department of Health and Human Services has a task force with representatives from the National Institute of Mental Health, the American Association of Suicidology, the American Psychological Association and the American Psychiatric Association. Congressman Gary Ackerman of New York has proposed a 30 million dollar measure to fund teen hot lines, suicide prevention programs for children, training courses for adults and public service announcements.

The *de facto* theoretician of the California suicide prevention movement is Charlotte Ross of San Mateo County's Crisis Center. She says: "Youngsters desperately want to know about suicide. Educators need to strip away the religious taboos surrounding youth suicide and replace the cloak of mystery with information that offers ways for adolescents to help both themselves and each other." Ross blasts adults who avoid frank discussions about suicide around youth. Such denial, she says, "is reminiscent of the earlier need to deny teenage sexuality and equally crippling in its implications." Parents are viewed in a peculiar light. In her state funded program, Ms. Ross follows a strategy where psychologists seek to create for teens in the schools "a supplemental or substitute family designed to facilitate growth." In other words, once again we have the family put-down and the professional stand-ins ready to replace them.

Most research on the subject points to the critical and positive role played by religious belief and practice and secure intact family structure as keys to preventing suicide.

a critical thinking activity

Recognizing Deceptive Arguments

People who feel strongly about an issue use many techniques to persuade others to agree with them. Some of these techniques appeal to the intellect, some to the emotions. Many of them distract the reader or listener from the real issues.

Most appeals can either advance an argument in an honest, reasonable way or they can deceive and distract readers from the real issues. It is important for critical thinkers to recognize these tactics in order to rationally evaluate an author's ideas. Here are a few common ones:

a. *bandwagon*—the idea that "everybody" does this or believes this

b. *deductive reasoning*—the idea that since a and b are true, c is also true, although there may not be a connection between a and c

c. *personal attack*—sharply criticizing an opponent personally instead of rationally debating his or her ideas

d. *scare tactic*—the threat that if you don't do this or believe this, something terrible will happen

e. *slanter*—trying to persuade through inflammatory and exaggerated language instead of through reason

f. *testimonial*—quoting or paraphrasing an authority or celebrity to support one's own viewpoint

Part I

Most of the statements below are taken from the viewpoints in this chapter. *Beside each one, mark the letter of the type of deceptive appeal being used. More than one type of tactic may be applicable. If you believe the statement is not any of the listed appeals, write N.*

1. Psychiatrists who support suicide education must be nuts to think that high schools can be a force for sanity in our mad society.

2. Discussions and increased awareness of suicide may actually put the idea of it into children's minds.

3. Each year, 100,000 children "accidentally" poison themselves. Since 88 percent of these children have a history of behavior problems and have alcholic or hostile parents, most of those poisonings are probably suicide attempts.

4. Practically everyone now accepts that educators must return to basics instead of trying to solve social problems.

5. Divorce and working mothers are to blame for youth suicide.

6. After 25 years of professional work in suicide prevention, I know from experience that preventing a suicide does not limit the suicidal person's freedom.

7. Just as I would not want to be trapped into a life that gave me no joy, so I would not want to mercilessly trap another by preventing his or her suicide.

8. Religion and the family are not mere options for us; they are necessary to prevent suicide and save lives.

9. Anyone with even a passing knowledge of the subject agrees that a great many deaths listed in the records as accidents or homicides are really suicides.

10. When we're depressed, we all need someone to listen to us, regardless of how old we are.

11. School social workers and psychologists keep themselves in business by exaggerating the teen suicide problem so the government will fund their suicide programs.

12. Suicide education classes require morose reading and unending discussions of students' attitudes toward death. It is no surprise that these depressing classes encourage teen suicide.

13. Typical American fathers spend "an average of 37 seconds a day with their children," according to an excellent study from the Department of Health and Human Services.

14. Professional help is needed when something as serious as suicide is considered.

15. Boys who are "sissies" and girls who are "tomboys" are more likely to attempt suicide than normal children who fit their proper, God-given sex roles.

Part II

Many of the viewpoints in this chapter use statistics to support their arguments. Statistics can also be deceptive. A writer may cite them in such a way that they *seem* to prove his point. Another writer might use the same statistics in her article to prove an opposite point.

For this part of the activity, break into small groups. Carefully study the four extracts listed below. First, list all the facts that the statistics in the extract seem to suggest. Second, discuss in your own words what the author is trying to prove. Finally, decide whether you believe the statistics actually support the author's argument.

1. Teenage suicides have climbed to epidemic proportions. The National Center for Health Statistics estimates that more than 6,000 people 16 to 24 years of age killed themselves in 1983.

2. The facts behind youth suicide suggest that the US does not face a growing problem. Even in 1975—the peak year for teen suicides—the total number among 15- to 19-year olds in a nation of 220 million people was 1,594. Since 1975 the numbers have stabilized.

3. Most suicidal teenagers do not really want to die. They want their parents to notice them. Nine out of ten teenage suicide attempts take place in the home. Seventy percent of teens who attempt suicide do so when their parents are home.

4. Suicide is now the second leading cause of death among young people 15-24. It is highly likely, therefore, that your school may have experienced the suicide of a student or an attempted suicide. It is also highly likely that some of the students in your school are struggling with feelings of sadness and depression that could lead them to consider suicide.

Periodical Bibliography

The following list of periodical articles deals with the subject matter of this chapter.

Aaron Beck — "When Hopelessness Sets In, Warns Psychiatrist Aaron Beck, Suicide Can Be Close Behind," *People,* April 7, 1986.

David R. Carlin Jr. — "Suicide and Private Morality," *America,* June 9, 1984.

George Howard Colt — "Suicide in America," *Reader's Digest,* January 1984.

Leon Eisenberg — "Does Bad News About Suicide Beget Bad News?" *The New England Journal of Medicine,* September 11, 1986.

John Leo — "Could Suicide Be Contagious?" *Time,* February 24, 1986.

Bruce A. Lipshy — "The Important Role of Business in Our Teenage Crisis," *Vital Speeches of the Day,* May 15, 1986.

Andrew H. Malcolm — "Some Elderly Choose Suicide Over Lonely, Dependent Life," *The New York Times,* September 24, 1984.

Ronald Maris — "Why 30,000 Americans Will Commit Suicide This Year," *U.S. News & World Report,* April 2, 1984.

Cynthia Pfeffer — "Teenage Suicide: Early-Warning Clues," *U.S. News & World Report,* March 31, 1986.

William E. Phipps — "Christian Perspectives on Suicide," *The Christian Century,* October 30, 1985.

Charlotte P. Ross — "Teaching Children the Facts of Life and Death," *Good Housekeeping,* July 1984.

Phyllis Schlafly — "Parents Speak Up Against Classroom Abuse," *The Phyllis Schlafly Report,* June 1985. Available from *The Phyllis Schlafly Report,* Box 618, Alton, IL 62002.

Steven Stack — "The Effect of Domestic/Religious Individualism on Suicide, 1954-1978," *Journal of Marriage and Family,* May 1985.

Lena Williams — "Out of Grief, A Drive To Cut Youth Suicide," *The New York Times,* November 11, 1985.

Is Infant Euthanasia Ever Justified?

death
and dying

"There are some infants who are human in the biological sense, but do not and never will possess any . . . 'indicators of humanhood.'"

Infant Euthanasia Is Sometimes Justified

Helga Kuhse and Peter Singer

In 1983 the journal *Pediatrics* published an article which provoked many strong reactions. The article, written by Peter Singer, concluded that some severely handicapped newborns had fewer human characteristics than some animals. The following viewpoint is an excerpt from the book *Should the Baby Live?*, written by Singer and his colleague Helga Kuhse. In it, they argue that infant euthanasia is justified for those infants who will never be able to live fully human lives because of their handicaps. Singer is a philosophy professor and director of the Centre for Human Bioethics at Monash University in Australia. Kuhse is a research fellow at the Centre.

As you read, consider the following questions:

1. What are the "indicators of humanhood" the authors discuss?
2. What point do Kuhse and Singer make by comparing human and animal life? What is your reaction to this comparison?
3. Why do the authors argue that infanticide does not threaten disabled adults?

People opposed to abortion or euthanasia often say that they believe in the sanctity of life. They almost never mean what they say. They do not mean, as their words seem to imply, that *all* life is sacred. If they did they would, presumably, make at least as much fuss about the daily slaughter of pigs, cattle, and chickens as they do about the much smaller number of foetuses killed by abortions. Yet most of those who say they believe in the sanctity of life are not vegetarians. Even if they were, to cut a living lettuce would still be contrary to a belief in 'the sanctity of life', taken literally. When people talk of their belief in the sanctity of life, it is the sanctity of *human* life that they really have in mind. . . .

All sanctity of life supporters agree upon the central claim: the killing of a human being is of unique moral significance.

Let us spell out one implication of this key claim. In saying that the killing of a human being is of unique moral significance, proponents of the sanctity of life principle are saying that to take the life of a human being—any human being—is in itself, and further consequences apart, far more momentous than taking the life of some other kind of being, for instance a chicken, pig, or cow. The principle of the sanctity of human life is a principle which serves to separate humans from non-human animals, and mark out human life for special attention. By comparison with the taking of human life, to take the life of a non-human animal is of relatively minor significance. The difference between killing a human and a non-human animal, according to this view, is not one of degree but of kind.

Defining "Human" Life

What could justify a sharp distinction in moral significance between taking human life and taking animal life? Only some relevant difference between the two groups. Many possible relevant differences might be suggested. Joseph Fletcher, a Protestant theologian, has listed some 'indicators of humanhood'. His list includes self-awareness, self-control, a sense of the future, a sense of the past, the capacity to relate to others, concern for others, communication, and curiosity. Other writers have emphasized rationality, the use of language, and autonomy. For our purposes it is not necessary to discuss which of these characteristics serve best to distinguish our own species from others. Many of them are related to others—one could not, for instance, have a sense of the past and future without at least some minimal degree of self-awareness and some capacity for rational thought. Taken as a cluster, these characteristics have undeniable moral significance.

90

It is entirely reasonable to suggest that it is much more serious to take the life of a being possessing all or most of these characteristics than it would be to take the life of a being possessing none of them.

Various grounds could be offered for saying that these characteristics are relevant to the seriousness of killing. Some people regard it as self-evident that the life of a rational, autonomous being is of greater value than the life of a being lacking these characteristics. Others focus especially on the capacity for self-awareness, and on the sense of the future. A self-aware being with a sense of the future can have hopes and desires about what might or might not happen to it in the future. To kill it is to prevent the fulfillment of these hopes and desires. This is a wrong which we cannot possibly do to a being that does not even understand that it exists as a separate being, with a past and a future.

"Human" vs. "Person"

So-called pro-life advocates equate "human" with "person" so as to confer the inviolability of persons onto the fetus. Similarly, newborns would count as persons possessing a right to life and assertable claims for protection. However, an equation of this sort seems misleading both with regard to the fetus and with regard to the neonate. To say that both are human is to make a biological, descriptive statement. No one denies that a fetus or a newborn is human. It is not a dog or cat fetus or newborn. The species of the fetus or newborn is not the point of disagreement in these debates. Rather, at issue is the value, the importance that being human has in the moral community. As philosopher Charles Hartshorne observes, "To short-circuit consideration of the value question by equating 'human' with 'human in the full value sense' [person] is not a scientific procedure but a political maneuver or semantic trick."

Earl E. Shelp, *Born To Die: Deciding the Fate of Critically Ill Newborns*, 1986.

Michael Tooley, an American philosopher now living in Australia, has developed this argument more systematically than anyone else. Tooley argues that only 'continuing selves' have a right to life. To be a continuing self it is not enough to have merely momentary desires or interests. Instead one must, at some time, be able to see oneself as existing over time. Thus only beings with a degree of self-awareness and a sense of the future can have a right to life. . . .

We have seen that the doctrine of the sanctity of life is really a doctrine about the sanctity of human life. We must now look at a crucial ambiguity in the term 'human'. When Joseph Fletcher called his list of characteristics 'indicators of humanhood', he meant that these characteristics were distinctive of human beings—the kind of things that mark out humans from all other animals. This is the sense given by the *Oxford English Dictionary* when it says that 'human' means 'having or showing the qualities or attributes proper to or distinctive of man'. It is the sense we have in mind when we say that an infant born without a brain is more like a vegetable than like a human being. There is, however, another sense of the term 'human' in which the infant born without a brain is, undeniably, a human being. This is the sense of 'human' which means, in effect, 'member of the species *Homo sapiens*'. In every cell of their bodies, the most grossly deformed infants born of human parents still possess the human genetic code. They are obviously not members of any other species. Therefore in the strict biological sense of the term they are human beings.

Species Membership

We have already seen that the first of these two senses of the term 'human' does refer to characteristics which are relevant to the moral significance of taking life; but what of the second sense, which draws the distinction between humans and others in terms of species membership alone? This distinction cannot be relevant to the moral significance of taking life. To claim that it is relevant is to make precisely the kind of claim made by the crude white racist who asserts that the killing of a black is less morally significant than the killing of a member of his own race. Like race or sex, species is not in itself a morally relevant characteristic.

Species might be indirectly morally relevant if it were a reliable indication of the possession of other, directly relevant capacities, such as those listed by Joseph Fletcher. But a moment's thought shows that this is not the case. . . . There are some infants who are human in the biological sense, but do not and never will possess any of Fletcher's 'indicators of humanhood'. Anencephalics—infants born with most of their brain missing— are in this category; so are infants who have suffered massive brain haemorrhages. Thus there are some who are humans in the sense of being members of the species *Homo sapiens* but not in the morally significant sense of having the distinctively human characteristics we have mentioned.

Is the converse also true? Are there some beings who possess the distinctive characteristics but are not members of the species *Homo sapiens*? This is more controversial. Certainly chimpanzees and gorillas show some degree of self-awareness. Washoe, the first chimpanzee to be taught sign language, was asked, as she was looking into a mirror, 'Who is that?' She made the signs for: 'Me, Washoe'. There is also good evidence that chimpanzees plan for the future. Jane Goodall, observing wild chimpanzees in Uganda, has given an account of how a lower-ranking chimpanzee who noticed a banana in a tree did not move directly towards the fruit, but instead went elsewhere until a higher-ranking chimpanzee had left the area; only then, some fifteen minutes later, did the first chimpanzee return and take the fruit.

Comparing Human and Animal Life

Just as some members of the species *Homo sapiens* do not possess the characteristics usually regarded as distinctive of our species, so there are some beings who are not members of our species who do appear to possess, at least to some degree, these characteristics. If we were simply to compare the characteristics of different individuals, irrespective of species, it is clear that we would have to go much further down the evolutionary scale before we reached a point at which non-human animals had capacities as limited as the most severely retarded humans. Not just chimpanzees, but also the animals we commonly kill for food—pigs, cows, and chickens—would compare favourably with anencephalic infants, or those who have suffered massive brain haemorrhages.

Newborns Are Not Persons

New-born humans are neither persons nor even quasi-persons, and their destruction is in no way intrinsically wrong. At about the age of three months, however, they probably acquire properties that are morally significant, and that make it to some extent intrinsically wrong to destroy them. As they develop further, their destruction becomes more and more seriously wrong, until eventually it is comparable in seriousness to the destruction of a normal adult human being.

Michael Tooley, *Abortion and Infanticide*, 1983.

Many people consider any such comparison of humans and animals to be offensive, but the facts cannot be denied and we gain nothing by pretending otherwise. Pigs, cows, and chickens have a greater capacity to relate to others, better ability to communicate, and far more curiosity, than the most severely retarded humans. Obviously there are gradations between the normal members of different species. Equally obviously, there are gradings within species, and especially within the human species. There is no clear-cut distinction between humans and other animals in respect of capacities like self-awareness, a sense of the past and future, or rationality. Instead there is an overlap: the best-endowed non-human animals rank well above those members of our species whose capacities are most limited. . . .

Now we can see what is wrong with the traditional principle of the sanctity of human life. Those who hold this principle invariably take 'human' in the strictly biological sense. They include within the scope of the principle all members of the species *Homo sapiens* and no members of any other species. The principle is 'speciest'; it is indefensible for the same reason that racism or sexism are indefensible. Those who hold the principle are giving great weight to something which is morally irrelevant—the species to which the being belongs. The traditional principle of the sanctity of human life elevates a morally insignificant characteristic into something of the utmost importance. . . .

The Stinson's Situation

Consider the situation in which Peggy Stinson found herself in December 1976. She was 24 weeks pregnant, but the pregnancy was going seriously wrong. The placenta was in the wrong position and threatening to detach altogether, causing a major haemorrhage that would put her life at risk as well as that of the baby. There was also a possibility of the baby's surviving, but with serious damage. Weighing up these difficulties on 15 December, Peggy and her husband Robert contemplated terminating the pregnancy. This would have reduced the risk to Peggy, and also ensured that they would not end up with a damaged baby. After the abortion, Peggy could have started on another pregnancy, with a high probability that it would develop normally. At 24 weeks, an abortion is legal in the United States; it would remain possible for Peggy to have an abortion for another two weeks.

In a single day, everything changed. On 16 December Peggy went into premature labour. The baby was born alive, but on the margins of viability. The Stinsons emphasized that they did not want any heroic measures taken. Nevertheless they gradually lost control of their child. Doctors threatened to take out court orders if the parents did not consent to treatment. The baby developed all sorts of complications. He was put on a respirator nonetheless. At one point there appeared to be a very real prospect that the hospital would hand over to the reluctant parents a living but grossly impaired child. This led Peggy to some ethical reflections. As she wrote in her diary:

> A woman can terminate a perfectly healthy pregnancy by abortion at 24½ weeks and that is legal. Nature can terminate a problem pregnancy by miscarriage at 24½ weeks and the baby must be saved at all cost; anything less is illegal and immoral. That's what they say at Pediatric Hospital, anyway.

Peggy Stinson was quite right to point out the oddity of this situation. After all, the mere location of the foetus or infant, whether inside or outside the womb, cannot make a crucial difference to its moral status. If the foetus at 24½ weeks does not have a right to life, why should we attribute such a right to the new-born baby at the same gestational age?

Opponents of abortion stress the similarities between the foetus and the infant, and urge that since the latter is clearly a human being, with the same right to life as any other human being, so the foetus should also be recognized as a human being with the same right to life as any other. We are not impressed, however, by the fact that both the infant and the foetus are clearly human beings. This is only true in the sense that they are members of the species *Homo sapiens*. Neither ranks as 'human' if judged against Fletcher's 'indicators of humanhood'. Neither is a person, as Locke and Tooley define the term. The new-born infant should therefore be regarded as we now regard the foetus, rather than the other way around.

Defective Infants

Once the religious mumbo-jumbo surrounding the term "human" has been stripped away, we may continue to see normal members of our species as possessing greater capacities of rationality, self-consciousness, communication, and so on, than members of any other species; but we will not regard as sacrosanct the life of each and every member of our species, no matter how limited its capacity for intelligent or even conscious life may be. If we compare a severely defective human infant with a nonhuman animal, a dog or a pig, for example, we will often find the nonhuman to have superior capacities, both actual and potential, for rationality, self-consciousness, communication, and anything else that can plausibly be considered morally significant.

Peter Singer, *Pediatrics*, July 1983.

In accepting abortion, as so many Western nations have now done, we have already taken a major step away from the traditional principle of the sanctity of human life. We have, however, come to place great weight on a boundary line—the moment of birth—that, while clear and precise, is not really crucial from the point of view of the moral status of the foetus or infant. The move to a less precise, but more significant boundary—the point at which there is self-awareness and a sense of the future—is therefore not as big a step as one might at first think.

No Slippery Slope

There is one further point about the dividing line we are proposing. It is sometimes said that if we start to kill severely handicapped infants we will end up threatening disabled adults as well. To allow infanticide before the onset of self-awareness, however, cannot threaten anyone who is in a position to worry about it. Anyone able to understand what it is to live or die must already be a person and has the same right to life as all the rest of us. Disability which does not rule out self-awareness and a sense of the future is totally irrelevant to the possession of the right to life.

Unlike many other forms of homicide, infanticide carried out by parents or with their consent poses no threat to anyone in the community who is capable of grasping what is happening. This fact goes a long way towards accounting for the equanimity with which many other cultures have accepted it. Nor is it only in other cultures that this point has been recognized. Jeremy Bentham, the founder of the reforming school of Utilitarians, criticized the severity with which infanticide was punished in his day, and remarked that the crime is 'of a nature not to give the slightest inquietude to the most timid imagination'. Infanticide threatens none of us, for once we are aware of it, we are not infants.

"The rights of some handicapped newborns are ignored because someone thinks their lives are not worth living."

Infant Euthanasia Is Never Justified

Melinda Delahoyde

Melinda Delahoyde was the former director of education of Americans United for Life. She has written many books, including *Fighting for Life: Defending the Handicapped Newborn's Right to Life.* In the following viewpoint, an excerpt from her book, she describes a change in doctors' attitudes. Many are no longer committed to treating conditions which can be corrected when the patient is a handicapped infant. Delahoyde argues that a doctor's job is to decide whether medical treatment will alleviate the child's condition; not to judge whether the child will live up to society's constantly changing standards of what attributes make someone a person.

As you read, consider the following questions:

1. Why does the author believe that the question of how doctors should treat handicapped infants is not as complex as some claim?
2. Why does Delahoyde think it is wrong to make value judgments about whether a handicapped child's life is worth living? What is your reaction to this argument?

From *Fighting for Life: Defending the Newborn's Right to Live,* © 1984 by Melinda Delahoyde. Published by Servant Publications, PO Box 8617, Ann Arbor, Michigan 48107. Used with permission.

On April 9, 1982, a baby boy known only as Baby Doe was born in Bloomington Hospital in Bloomington, Indiana. The baby, the parents' third child, was diagnosed at birth as having Down's Syndrome. He also had a badly formed esophagus which required an immediate operation. Without this operation, which is successful more than 90 percent of the time, the baby would be unable to digest nourishment and would die.

Pediatricians consulting on the case advised immediate surgery. But the parents, after consulting with their obstetrician, refused the surgery for their infant. They knew this would mean death for him, but they were convinced their child, born with Down's Syndrome, had no chance for a meaningful human life. Their decision was final. . . .

As Baby Doe's lawyers raced against the clock, pediatricians in the Bloomington hospital tried to convince the parents to let them operate. The baby, now starving, had been transferred to a private room on another floor because the nurses in the newborn nursery could not stand to hear the cries of this dying newborn child. . . .

Infanticide Is Widespread

Baby Doe's death was a clearcut case of infanticide. Infanticide is the killing of an infant by direct or indirect means. Baby Doe was killed by the intentional neglect of his parents and doctors at the hospital. A child who had every chance to live was killed by those who thought his life was not worth living.

Many Americans heard the word "infanticide" for the first time in connection with the Baby Doe case. Yet for years doctors had been aiding the deaths of handicapped newborn babies—babies who were not born dying, but who needed help to live. Baby Doe was only one of hundreds, perhaps thousands, of children who never survived the newborn nursery. . . .

Abortion and Infanticide

Events do not happen in a vacuum; infanticide did not just suddenly appear on the American scene. Ideas have consequences, and ideas about the low value of human life took root in our culture long before Infant Doe was killed in Bloomington. Infanticide is the logical conclusion of a mindset that casually allows the destruction of more than 1.6 million unborn children every year.

Abortion leads to infanticide. In 1973 the Supreme Court told us that some human lives, the unborn, were not worth protecting under the law. Some human beings can be destroyed at the mother's word. But if the unborn can be destroyed because they

98

are unplanned or imperfect, then why not destroy a newborn child for the very same reasons. After all, what is the difference between taking a human life three days before birth and taking that same life three days after birth? There is no real difference except that before birth we call it "abortion" and after birth, "infanticide.". . .

Nowhere is this progression from abortion to infanticide more clearly illustrated than in the words of doctors themselves. In 1973, *California Medicine*, a leading medical journal, published their now-famous editorial about abortion and medical ethics. That editorial plainly acknowledged that abortion was the taking of a human life and noted that our society could justify this killing only by calling it something else. It concluded that society takes such pains to justify the killing because we had accepted the idea that some human lives weren't worth living.

Doctors' Duty To Heal

The doctors are there to heal, not to make qualitative decisions about where someone might be in 10 years. They have the skill to operate. . . . So operate. Treat the baby. That's all we parents ask. Give us the burden, and let people take care of their own lives.

Veronica Donnelly, quoted in *The Washington Times*, July 10, 1984.

Ten years later, *Pediatrics*, the leading journal for pediatricians, published a similar commentary [by Peter Singer]. This time the subject was newborn human life and medical ethics. In the author's words:

If we compare a severely defective human infant with a dog or a pig . . . we will often find the nonhuman to have superior capacities . . . Only the fact that the defective infant is a member of the species *Homo sapiens* leads it to be treated differently from the dog or pig. But species membership alone is not relevant. . . . If we can put aside the obsolete and erroneous notion of the sanctity of all human life, we may start to look at human life as it really is: at the quality of life that each human being has or can attain.

In other words, human life isn't special. We should compare our children to pigs and dogs and whoever comes out ahead is allowed to survive. We have moved one step further in the devaluation of human life. Ten years ago the quality of life world view gave us abortion on demand. Today that same mind-set brings us infanticide. . . .

The extent of the medical profession's shift from a sanctity of life perspective to a quality of life value system was shown in a national poll in 1977 of the attitudes of pediatricians and pediatric surgeons. Almost seventy-seven percent of pediatric surgeons and sixty percent of pediatricians responding said they would go along with a parent's decision to refuse surgery for a child with an intestinal obstruction if that child also had Down's Syndrome. Almost twenty-four percent would encourage parents to refuse their consent for treatment. Less than four percent would go to court, against the parents' wishes, to obtain an order to treat the child. In cases where parents and physicians had agreed to let a baby die, almost sixty-four percent of the pediatric surgeons would hasten the process by stopping all nourishment and supportive care for the baby.

We need to understand what we are talking about here. Three fourths of the nation's pediatric surgeons who responded would refuse a life-saving operation for a handicapped child. This is not a child born dying, but rather a child who has every chance for a life filled with hope and love. This is a child who will most likely be able to read, write, and may be able to take a job. Only a tiny percentage of those surgeons surveyed (3.4 percent) would try to obtain a court order to treat the baby. . . .

Infanticide is now a feature of American life. Some handicapped babies are being denied treatment. Some are literally starved to death in the name of "love" and "compassion." Doctors who have been devoted to the care and healing of our sick are now becoming death dealers for those whose lives are not "worthy to be lived." A society once known for its loving concern for its most helpless members now kills its unborn and even newborn children.

Many said, "It can't happen here." They were wrong. It is happening here. The death of our handicapped babies moves us several steps further down on the slippery slope of planned death for all those who don't measure up to our always changing standards of what it means to be a person.

Clarifying the Issue

Misconceptions and distortions continue to surround the issue of infanticide even as it basks in the glare of sudden publicity. Some medical decisions about handicapped infants are genuinely complex. Not every decision to withhold or withdraw treatment from a critically ill child is infanticide.

Indeed, the medical complexity of a particular child's situation can keep us from a clear overview of exactly what is happening in American hospitals. Pro-infanticide advocates often dwell on the complexity of a particular case in order to introduce the idea that the issue is so complex that there are *no* clear-cut principles to guide our decision-makers. In fact, there are clear guidelines we must follow to protect innocent human lives. Let's clarify the issue.

Many people do not understand the difference between committing infanticide and choosing not to prolong the death of an infant. Doctors have always made choices to discontinue a useless treatment or not to begin a treatment that will not benefit the patient. If no known medical treatment will improve a handicapped child's chances for life, then no treatment should be given. If the child is born with so many anomalies that the case is *medically* hopeless, and there is no prognosis for recovery and future life, then again treatment is not required. In short, doctors are not obligated to prolong the death process by providing useless treatment. Doctors who do not treat in these situations are not committing infanticide.

Making Treatment Decisions

Dr. C. Everett Koop, our nation's Surgeon General and a leading pediatric surgeon, has written of his own experiences with terminally ill youngsters. He writes:

> I happen to believe that the terminal patient ... for example should be permitted to die as quietly and in a dignified manner as possible rather than to use every conceivable combination of chemotherapeutic agents for the prolongation of life without alleviation of the disease.

This is the morally correct way to treat a dying child. Unnecessary treatment is not demanded. To refuse to give useless treatment is a truly compassionate form of care for a dying patient. By contrast, victims of infanticide are infants who are *not* dying but are nevertheless refused care. There is an accepted medical treatment that can be given these children, but they are denied the treatment only because they are handicapped.

Down's Syndrome Children

> My son Christopher, like most Down's children I know, is a delightful, functional, sentient person who feels joy, sadness, love, satisfaction, and frustration as keenly as his normal siblings. He is, to be sure, "different"—in physical appearance, in capacity for scholarly pursuits, and in his congenital inability to hate. I cannot believe that he, or the world, would have been better off if his pediatrician had written a death sentence for him in the doctor's order book on the day of his birth.

Louis Lasagna, *Human Life Review*, Spring 1984.

This is the heart of the infanticide debate. No one is demanding that a baby be kept alive at all costs when the child has no chance for life. No one is telling doctors to put aside their best medical judgments in order to give a child a treatment they think is useless. The problem comes when physicians stray outside their field of expertise—medicine—and make value judgments about

101

the *worth* of a child's life that have nothing to do with the baby's medical condition. . . .

Children deserve to live, and they should receive available and appropriate treatments. The situation becomes "complex" only when we begin weighing the value of the child's life against other factors like the parents' preferences and the financial cost of caring for the baby. "Complexity" is often a smokescreen to hide the kind of thinking going on here. The baby's right to life becomes only one of many rights that must be "weighed and measured." Sometimes the right to life comes out on top and the baby lives. Sometimes not. . . .

Another way of obscuring the issue is to emphasize the parents' heartbreak and their agonizing decision without reference to the rights of a helpless baby. Parents do face a difficult and emotionally stressful time when their child is born handicapped. But they are not the only ones who suffer. The child endures the death sentence. But media reports focus only upon the grief and agony of the parents. This redirects our attention from the true victim of nontreatment—the newborn baby.

Equal Protection Under the Law

Advocating a child's right to medically indicated treatment is not a complex request. It is simple and basic. It is something that no one would have questioned several years ago. We are asking for the right of every child, no matter how severely handicapped, to be treated exactly as a "normal" child would be. Handicapped children should be given the same medical treatment that would bring relief and healing. We are asking that a child not be denied treatment simply because he or she is handicapped.

How strange it is that we should have to fight so hard for something that most of us take for granted—our protection as human beings under the law. Everyone is supposed to be equally protected under our legal system. Everyone is suppose to have access to care and treatment. Yet the rights of some handicapped newborns are ignored because someone thinks their lives are not worth living.

"Ultimately, the entire crushing weight of such life-and-death decision making falls on . . . the mother and father of the infant involved."

Parents Should Decide When Infant Euthanasia Is Justified

B.D. Colen

One of the major issues in the infant euthanasia debate is who should decide what medical care critically ill infants should receive. Author B.D. Colen contends that parents should make these life and death decisions. Colen, the science editor of *Newsday*, was co-author of a Pulitzer Prize-winning 1984 *Newsday* series on the *Baby Jane Doe* case. In the following viewpoint, he examines two cases involving handicapped infants. In both cases, the parents had to live on a day-to-day basis with the consequences of the treatment decisions they made. Colen concludes that the fair way to handle infant euthanasia is to let parents decide.

As you read, consider the following questions:

1. Why does the author oppose federal interference in cases involving handicapped newborns?
2. How has society treated deformed infants in the past, according to Colen?

When Bob and Marty Bailey go for a walk, strangers often approach to take a peek at what's inside the Perego twin stroller that Marty pushes along in front of her. "They always come up and say, 'Oh, let me see the ba—' and they blanch and turn away," Bob said.

Nearly everyone does blanch at the first sight of Bob and Marty's daughter, Cara Lynn. Bob himself just "stood there and cried" the first time he saw Cara. But then, what parent, or what person for that matter, is prepared for the first view of what the dictionary describes as an "anencephalic monster," an infant born with no cerebral cortex and, in Cara's case, a skull that looks as though it has been sawed off about two inches above eyelids that are fused shut?

When Bob and Marty saw their child the first time after her birth, they didn't even notice many of Cara's other deformities.

They noticed the cleft lip, which opens all the way into her right nostril. They could see the hollow eye sockets, covered with the fused lids and extraordinarily lush lashes. They could see that her ears didn't match and were set too low on her head.

But she wearing a hospital cap, so they couldn't see the fluid-filled, bluish and mottled pink membrane covering the top of her head. And she was wrapped in a blanket, so they couldn't see that some of her fingers were fused together and some were missing. They couldn't tell that one arm was functionally no more than a flipper. They were unaware that she had a malformed clavicle and a deformed hip. They wouldn't see the deformed toes and club foot until they later unwrapped the blanket. They had no way of knowing that, in fact, the only symmetrical parts of her body were her two perfectly formed thumbs.

And they didn't know then that she was alive only in the most rudimentary sense, unable ever to function on more than a reflexive, primitive, nonsentient level. . . .

After Cara's Birth

Marty was discharged from the hospital within twenty-four hours of the delivery, and she and Bob went home to be together. Bob had been told to make funeral arrangements for Cara, whose name had been picked out long before her delivery. The couple had told the physicians at the Catholic hospital that they didn't want any extraordinary means or any technology used to extend Cara's life. "I had the impression that my wife was the living one and Cara was going to be the dying one," Bob said, explaining that he somehow had been led to believe that Cara's death was assured,

"but I don't know where I got that impression." But for
the couple was told not to visit their daughter, not to get a
They'd call to check on her condition and be told there
change.

Finally, they could stand it no longer, said Bob, and the
to visit her for the first time. Then, as the days became
the couple at first began visiting every two days, and then
day. They were becoming attached in spite of themselves. T
read Cara's chart when they went in and would note that o
shifts she didn't seem to be getting her regular feedings, f
that often took more than two hours because her cleft li
it impossible for her to suck properly. "We'd ask them, 'D
mean you didn't feed her, or you just didn't put it dow
we just didn't put it down,'" Marty recalled being told

Overruled and Dismissed

[Dr.] Carvalho had taken over [our] baby. He would treat
according to his ideas about what was right even though
see that his moral or religious views differed drastically f
He could overrule us, could—and did—dismiss what w
automatically, unemotionally, as if we were beneath notic
he has the power.

Peggy Stinson, *The Long Dying of Baby Andrew*, 1983.

The end of the hospital stay finally came when B
arrived one day to visit Cara and found her lying
a bottle propped in her mouth, choking on formula
ing down her face. The next day the couple took t
home. "We decided that if she was going to live
twelve weeks, what ever extraordinary time, she d
of love with her parents, not in the hands of deta
sionals. We decided to have a baby and we had a bab

While bringing Cara home may have been "bes
assuming that she could benefit from more loving car
is a big assumption—it condemned Marty to what she
describe a year and a half later as a life of "shift wo
had decided to speak with me then because she was s
by the much publicized Baby Doe case on Long Island
which the Reagan adminstration, spurred on by so-c
to-life organizations, was fighting to obtain the medic
of a deformed infant at a local hospital. "There's nob
me," she said then. "Where are they?" she asked of
who would force parents and physicians to save every
matter how damaged. "They step into a life, do their
good-bye. . . . These people save a life, clap their hands

105

then they turn away."

ly, at the same time the administration was fighting un-
ully to force surgery for one defective infant, the Baileys
hting to convince Medicaid that they deserved help for
. . The infant's head dressings, which cost more than $600
h, had to be changed every two hours. She had to be spoon-
ery three hours. Her diapers had to be changed constantly,
would for the rest of her life. Marty couldn't find baby-
ho were either willing or capable of caring for the infant.
ew occasions when the parents tried to hire a licensed
nurse to care for Cara, the woman would generally leave
shift and never return. . . .

id did finally agree to help the Baileys, but only after
atened to institutionalize Cara, which the government
e had to pay for and which would be far more expen-
home care. . . . Federal and state taxpayers are paying
$43,000 a year to maintain the life of a child who has
reness, let alone an ability to receive and return love.
ll this, Bob and Marty Bailey love their daughter. . . .
her enough to let her go," Bob said, "which to me is
e kind of love. We're not to the point of loving her so
we want her to live a life that I can't really consider

about how they will react when she dies.
very sad," Marty concluded, "and it will be a great

A Candidate for Infanticide

ment of her birth, Cara Lynn Bailey was a candidate
. In fact, it is not an exaggeration to say that what
not that she might have been killed but that she
ebody didn't do his job," a noted neonatologist said
told about Cara. "She should never have left the
." Indeed, it is not at all uncommon when a baby
orn for the physician to place the infant in a tray
of the delivery room and simply cover the tray with
walk away. In a short time the infant is dead and the
told that the mother delivered a stillborn, badly
infant. . . .

ut recorded history, and undoubtedly earlier, babies
defects have been killed or left to die. While we can
y recall an elementary school teacher telling us in
nes that the Spartans left deformed infants on moun-
e were less likely to be told, or to remember from our
at Plato's *Republic*, one of the philosophical blueprints
civilizations, advocates killing defective newborns. . . .
ly a combination of economic security and modern

Duane C. Barnhart, for Greenhaven Press.

medical technology that has given today's "civilized" societies the luxury of vigorously seeking to protect the severely deformed from what is actually part of the process of natural selection. But as medical skill and technology have developed to the point where infants with major birth defects can be saved, parents and physicians have been forced for the first time to confront the difficult choice of whether or not to save severely deformed newborns. . . .

On October 11, 1983, . . . a baby girl was born in St. Charles Hospital in Port Jefferson, New York, who would come to symbolize all the dilemmas involved in the Baby Doe issue. Baby Jane

Doe, as she was first publicly known, was suffering from a constellation of birth defects, including meningomyelocele (a failure of a portion of the neural tube to form properly, thus exposing an area of spinal cord in her lower back), a malformed left foot, paralysis of the legs, anal incontinence, mild hydrocephalus, microcephaly (an abnormally small head, and thus an abnormally small brain, for her size) and certain facial characteristics indicative of retardation.

Initially unaware of any problem other than the meningomyelocele, the parents authorized their daughter's transfer to University Hospital at Stony Brook, a state teaching hospital. It is unlikely we will ever really know who told what to whom during those first few days at Stony Brook, but after initially signing an authorization for anesthesia for surgery, the parents refused to authorize the surgery necessary to close the opening in their daughter's back. As he later testified in court, neurologist George Newman, who examined the infant, believed that "on the basis of the combinations of the malformations that are present in this child she is not likely to ever achieve any meaningful interactions with her environment, nor ever to achieve any interpersonal relationships that we consider human, and that she is capable of experiencing pain." Newman further testified that because he believed the infant had "only limited ability to experience comfort, and primarily an ability to experience pain, to perform this surgery would increase the total pain that the child would experience. There are complications of the [meningomyelocele], including urinary tract infections, skin infections, edema of the legs, and numerous other conditions, all of which would produce pain and none of which might be detectable before they produce pain in the child." Not surprisingly, the parents refused to authorize what they were told would be life-extending surgery to close the spinal defect. . . .

Outside Interference

It would have been difficult enough for the parents, physicians and nurses caring for this Baby Doe had they simply had to live with the decision that had been made and care for the infant. . . . But those caring for Baby Jane Doe had more to worry about than whether they made the right choice for her: On Saturday, October 15, just four days after the infant's birth, New York Supreme Court Justice Frank DeLuca, Vermont attorney and zealous right-to-life advocate Lawrence Washburn, an assistant Suffolk County district attorney and another private attorney appeared at University Hospital for a "brief, off-the-record, judicial inquiry" into the case of Baby Jane Doe. As soon as he managed to contact the attorney for the university, the administrator on duty at the hospital sent the four men packing, politely telling them to file a formal complaint if they had anything to discuss. . . .

The parents and the hospital were upheld by the courts at every stage. New York state's highest court held that the case did not belong in the courts in the first place because the legislature had intended that such issues be dealt with by state agencies utilizing the child protection statutes. . . .

Inaccurate Medical Assessment

While the parents had decided not to authorize the closing of the spinal opening, which would drastically reduce the chances of life-threatening infections, and refused to authorize the insertion of a shunt to drain fluid from the skull and reduce the chances of further brain damage, they did authorize the use of antibiotics to fight the infections the baby quickly developed. . . . The parents visited their infant, whom they had named Kery-Lynn, every day over the months she was in the newborn intensive care unit of University Hospital, obviously becoming more and more attached to her. Finally, when she was about five months old, they authorized the insertion of the shunt whose insertion outsiders had attempted to compel five months earlier.

One of the ironies in the case is that the original medical testimony looks less and less accurate as time passes. By six months, the infant who would never be responsive was cooing and carrying on with obvious pleasure at bath time. By a year she was reportedly functioning on about a six-month level, responding to her parents, grasping at objects, enjoying toys. Would she ever progress beyond that level? That is another question. But an even more important question is, would she progress further had her spinal defect been closed and a shunt been inserted shortly after birth? The obvious answer to that question would seem to be yes. In matters such as this, however, every answer seems to pose a question, which in this case is: Does the fact that she might have done better had surgery been performed mean that surgery should have been performed?

A strong argument can be made that this was the "wrong" Baby Doe to be the central figure in a precedent-setting case. A case involving an infant like Cara Lynn Bailey, who possesses none of the attributes and abilities we equate with personhood and humanity, would have made the issues far clearer, the lines far easier to draw. But isn't the very point of the Baby Doe question that there are no easy answers? . . . Each case leaves another set of parents wondering if they made the right choices, whether they withheld medical treatment—or authorized it. Ultimately, the entire crushing weight of such life-and-death decision making falls on two persons, the mother and the father of the infant involved. Once the baby either dies or goes home, the case ends for the physicians and nurses involved. They may think about it once in a while, they may even have a nightmare or two, but they do not live with the decision on a daily basis. They do not have to live with knowing that they decided that *their* child would be better off dead. Or, alternately, they do not have to care for a severely handicapped child for the rest of their lives. The physicians and nurses are not the ones who have to fight with the state and federal bureaucracies for every penny of the often inadequate aid the parents of such an infant receive. If the child is eventually institutionalized, the physicians and nurses do not have to go to the institution, to be bowled over by the stench of urine and disinfectant, to see a wholly inadequate number of attendants attempting to care for the castoffs of society. And, of course, the right-to-life advocates who would save every infant, no matter how badly deformed or hopelessly retarded, are, in the vast majority of cases, nowhere to be seen except on picket lines and in court. . . .

Let the Parents Decide

There have always been mechanisms for protecting the helpless and making sure that the traditional medical decision-making process is not abused. Perhaps decisions involving the care of hopelessly ill and defective newborns should be left to those traditional processes, to parents and physicians who do the best they can under difficult circumstances. Until such time as society is willing to pay the bill for truly humane institutions or twenty-four-hour home care for all such infants, to offer families alternatives other than death or living death, shouldn't these decisions be left to those who will have to live with them?

"[For] the 'child's best interest'. . . one cannot assume that the best representative is the parents."

Parents Alone Should Not Make Infant Euthanasia Decisions

Charles Krauthammer

In the following viewpoint Charles Krauthammer, a well-known columnist and senior editor at *The New Republic*, considers the issues involved in infant euthanasia decisions. Krauthammer argues that promoting the child's best interest should be the basis for any decision. Parents cannot be expected to be selfless and divorce their own interests from the child's interests, he writes, and doctors sometimes allow other considerations to influence their judgment regarding treatment. For those reasons, Krauthammer argues, federal involvement is beneficial and necessary.

As you read, consider the following questions:

1. Why does the author argue that infant euthanasia decisions should be based on the child's best interest?
2. What are the arguments against "Big Brother" interference in Baby Doe cases? How does Krauthammer refute these arguments?
3. Does the author believe that all lives are worth living?

Charles Krauthammer, "What To Do About 'Baby Doe,'" *The New Republic*, September 2, 1985. Reprinted by permission of THE NEW REPUBLIC, © 1985, The New Republic, Inc.

If physicians are going to play God . . . let us hope they play God as God plays God.

Paul Ramsey

Between 1977 and 1982 a group of Oklahoma doctors conducted an experiment on children born with spina bifida. Spina bifida is a congenital malformation in which the spine does not close and is often exposed through the skin. It can lead to paralysis, retardation, and other disabilities. Before treatment became available in the early 1960s, the condition was almost universally fatal. The purpose of the experiment was to determine which spina bifida newborns to treat and which to let die. Doctors divided the infants into two groups. Those with a more favourable prognosis for a good "quality of life" were selected for immediate and aggressive treatment (surgery to close the spine, shunting water away from the brain, antibiotics). All of these babies survived. The other groups of infants deemed to have a poor "quality of life" prognosis was selected for no treatment at all. Parents demanded treatment anyway for five of them, and three survived. Of the rest, all 24 died within 189 days. . . .

The doctors and the hospital were threatened with a suit by groups representing the disabled and by the ACLU. The charge was discrimination against the more severely affected children. They were denied treatment because they were deemed to be not worth saving. That they were not medically beyond saving was shown by the survival of three of the five whose parents insisted on treatment even though they were chosen to die. The non-treatment decision proceeds from "a eugenic premise," writes Martin Gerry in the July [1985] issue of *Law and Medicine,* "not . . . that a child cannot or will not live, but . . . that the child should not live."

Different Conclusions

The remarkable thing about the clash between baby doctor and baby advocate—and an indication of the gulf of incomprehension that separates them—is that there was no need for daring undercover work here. The doctors published their study in the October 1983 issue of *Pediatrics,* one of their profession's leading journals. They clearly felt they had nothing to hide. The Oklahoma doctors consider what they did to be accepted, if novel, practice. The baby advocates call it euthanasia. Or, as one of their cause's most prominent propagandists, Nat Hentoff, likes to say: murder. How can reasonable people come to such wildly different conclusions? To start with, the doctors pretend to too much reasonableness.

The tone of their article, a tone of unrelieved moral flatness, seems designed to provoke indignation if not litigation. "The 'untreated survivor' has not been a significant problem in our experience," they write. "All 24 babies who have not been treated at all have died at an average of 37 days." Success. Their description of the "selection process" is casual, lacking the slightest awareness of the awful historical echoes associated with that term. And their moral calculus is so technologically streamlined that it yields results like: "Whatever decision the parents make, it is important that they be relieved of any sense of guilt." Any decision?

Still, you don't, or shouldn't, get hauled into court for transgressions of tone. You get hauled in for murder. Was this murder? There is a real question here: If we must make life-and-death decisions on behalf of others, can we ever morally choose death?

Life Worse than Death

Is there a life worse than death? Judging from how adults act and talk, yes. Voluntary death is not an irrational response of people to intractable pain, or imprisonment, or dishonor, for example. (There is even a large body of opinion that would add communism to the list.) We do not assume that life is automatically the supreme value. In deciding for ourselves whether there is a life worse than death we would weigh the costs and the benefits of continued existence. But in deciding for others, as we do for a newborn, the first question is: Whose costs and whose benefits? Whose interests count: society's, the family's, or the patient's?

Children Are Not Property

"The right to decide who will live or die is the essence of slavery," Robert D'Agastino, a former Justice Department attorney, said. "And, if there is a private right to decide a child will die, whether that right is left in the hands of a hospital, a doctor or his parents, then that child is nothing more than a piece of property."

Carlton Sherwood, *The Washington Times*, July 11, 1984.

The societal consideration goes something like this: we are a vast society with vast needs and scarce resources. Even scarcer resources are allocated to medicine. The cost of saving and maintaining a sickly child (or adult, as Governor Richard D. Lamm of Colorado, has argued) is huge. That money could be better spent saving and sustaining many others. As Lamm put it to the elderly some years ago, at some point "we all have a duty to die" and make room for others.

This idea usually goes by the name of triage, and has almost no application to "Baby Doe" disabled newborns. For one thing,

113

in their treatment, resources are not scarce. They are a tiny number every year, and the reason that they are not treated vigorously is to spare them or their families anguish, not to spare the country respirators. Second, even if there were a shortage, it is one thing to tell the elderly to drop dead. They can weigh the invitation and choose. An infant chooses nothing. He is at our mercy. And mercy—and justice—dictate that in deciding whether he is to live or die, the federal deficit not enter the calculation.

The Child's Best Interest

Generally, however, a different calculation is made. When families and their doctors decide not to treat a defective newborn, they are not balancing society's costs and benefits, but the family's. That includes, of course, the newborn's, but also those of the rest of the family: siblings, parents, even the "marriage" itself.

Now, these are not frivolous considerations. But they cannot be morally relevant to a decision about the life or death of a child. That idea commands a remarkable consensus in the ethical literature. The President's Commission for the Study of Ethical Problems in Medicine, for example, declares that any criteria for non-treatment must "exclude consideration of the negative effects of an impaired child's life on other persons, including parents, siblings, and society." Family members can and should be made to yield certain goods to accommodate other family members. They cannot be made to yield their lives.

In weighing life against death for a child, therefore, there is no place for the utilitarian calculations of others. It is impermissible to add the interests of society or even the family to the scale. The only standard is the child's own best interest.

Who is to represent that interest? An immediate corollary of the "child's best interest" standard is that one cannot assume that the best representative is the parents. There is a widespread assumption that parents should make unmolested life-or-death decisions for their children because they act as the child's proxy. They don't. No matter how well intentioned, parents cannot disentangle their own best interests and that of their family from that of the newborn. Nor can the doctor. He has the parents, the family, and his own profession to think of.

The Need for Big Brother

That is why there is need for Big Brother, as both *The New York Times* and *The Wall Street Journal* derisively called federal intrusion into the nurseries of the country to try to prevent non-treatment of handicapped newborns.

The complaint against Big Brother usually takes three forms. First is the claim that "decisions about a child's medical care" (as the *Times* describes what was at stake in a 1983 spina bifida case on Long Island) should be left to parents and doctors. This claim rests on a linguistic sleight of hand. What is being decided in a spina bifida case is not which medical treatment is most likely to benefit the child, but whether life itself will benefit the child. Once the latter decision is made, the medical treatment is straight-forward. The question is not how to preserve a life, but whether. The first is a medical question; the second, a moral one. To confuse the two is to engage in what Robert Veatch of Georgetown University's Kennedy Institute of Ethics calls "medicalizing value choices." Neither doctors nor parents, nor doctors and parents together, have a special moral sense.

A second defense of parental autonomy rests on "privacy." But in a society where child labor, child abuse, and even withholding a child from school have been deemed a legitimate concern of government, it is absurd to claim privacy for decisions about life and death.

The final defense of parental autonomy, therefore, is the notion that the parents are the child's true proxy. But it is simply false to assume that they necessarily act in the child's best interest. To ask that of a parent is to demand a rare degree of selflessness. Sainthood is not easy to mandate and it should not be the basis for policy. . . .

Abuses of Babies' Rights

In practice, I contend that decisions about resuscitation are not usually based on consideration of the wishes of the infant at all, but rather on the inconvenience, suffering, and expense to be borne by the parents, the doctors, the hospital, and the government. The Baby Doe rules came about because of abuses of babies' rights— not as a barrier against their rights.

David C. Miller, *The New England Journal of Medicine*, September 11, 1986.

The "child's best interests" standard . . . rules out deciding life or death on the basis of society's needs (triage) or on the basis of the family's. As a corollary, it rules out relying solely on parents as proxies. But saying that the surgeon general or a hospital ethics committee or a guardian *ad litem* should superintend any parental decision only opens the argument. Whoever decides, how are they to decide? What *is* the child's best interests?

Death Is Sometimes Best

Specifically, can it ever be death? We know from the action of sentient adults that the answer can be yes in at least two medical contexts: patients with intractable pain and patients who are dying and for whom all that medicine can offer is heroic and pointless prolongation of the process. These are easy cases. Consider a difficult case. Consider a patient who has severe spina bifida, resulting in paralysis, retardation, and recurrent medical illness. Consider, in other words, those babies in the Oklahoma experiment. What are their best interests? The President's Commission concludes that "permanent handicaps justify a decision not to provide life-sustaining treatment only when they are so severe that continued existence would not be a net benefit to the infant." "Net benefit" suggests those cost/benefit, quality-of-life considerations that the Baby Doe advocates so vociferously oppose. It sounds like a very liberal criterion. Except, adds the commission, that "the surrogate is obligated to try to evaluate benefits and burdens from the infant's own perspective."

The implications of this last condition are enormous. For adults who have known otherwise, spina bifida or some other severe disability might be considered a fate worse than death. But the child will have known nothing else. He must compare spina bifida not against normal life but against no life. If we are enjoined to make a decision from his point of view, it seems we must always choose life. . . .

A Relative Good

This cannot be right. . . . Philosopher Richard McCormick [writes], . . . "Life is a relative good, and the duty to preserve it a limited one. . . . It is not that "some lives are valuable, others not," says McCormick. "Of course [the individual] has, or is, a value. The only point is whether this undoubted value has any potential at all, in continuing physical survival, for attaining a share, even if reduced, in the 'higher, more important good.'" . . .

Giving absolute primacy to life is meant to keep us from the slippery slope, but unfortunately life takes place there. If you believe that life is a divine gift, which man has no right to refuse, that is one thing. But it is difficult to accept the secular argument that no deprivation of human endowment could ever warrant the choice not to perpetuate life. If there is no relatedness, no human context for life, then it is hard to see where the "best interest" criterion is violated. I could produce (and you could imagine) a hypothetical example so awful—so awful that I cannot bring myself to write it—as to empty the "best interest" standard of any meaning. . . .

Even according to McCormick's criteria—a potential for relationships and development—the Oklahoma spina bifida babies did not warrant non-treatment. Since the 1960s, aggressive treatment has kept alive a large number of spina bifida children. And more than just kept alive. Only 30 percent of them are retarded. Even those with hydrocephalus, one of the conditions that apparently led the Oklahoma doctors to categorize a baby for non-treatment (though the criteria are never made explicit), have a better than

50 percent chance for being intellectually normal if they are treated reasonably early and do not develop meningitis. . . .

The final regulations issued by the Department of Health and Human Services in May 1985 . . . establish strict criteria for nontreatment. . . .Treatment may be withheld only if it will prolong dying or cause too much suffering. . . .

Parental Desires

Handicapped infants must not be denied health care simply because their parents do not want it. . . . Parental desires should never be the criteria used to determine whether a handicapped infant should live or die.

Kerby Anderson, Dallas *Morning News*, November 11, 1983.

The rule, the suit, the debate, the fuss make me perversely optimistic. It is commonplace to claim that as our society has become more technologically advanced we have become less and less sensitive to the value of human life: the technological imperative—an imperative for cleanliness, physical perfection, and ease—has made us insensitive to those human beings who don't fit the mold. Conservatives argue that society is conveniently disposing of those infirm at either end of life whose continued existence is a burden on society. I think not, or at least not more so than in other times. In previous ages, infant mortality was so high that it bred a certain callousness about the value of early life. Historian Joseph Kett writes: ''Parents left their infants alone for long periods, seem to have been indifferent to their welfare, could not even remember their names, refused to attend the funerals of children under five, routinely farmed infants out for wet nursing, and argued in divorce proceedings, not over which parent could have the infant, but over which could send it packing.'' As for the severely deformed newborns, these were known as ''monsters,'' and since ''monsters were not [considered] human,'' says Kett, ''their destruction was not viewed as murder.'' This is not just ancient history. It is reported that in England the rate of stillbirth of babies with spina bifida was 40 percent in 1958 and zero percent in 1962. It was between those two dates that treatment of the condition became possible. The stillbirths were almost certainly not stillbirths. They were obstetric euthanasia.

In fact, ours is a society enormously attentive to those in the dawn, the twilight, and the shadow of life, as Hubert Humphrey used to describe the young, the old, and the sick. And it is becoming increasingly attentive to the disabled newborn, who is all three. The Oklahoma doctors are learning that right now.

117

"As her own person under the Constitution, . . . [Baby Jane Doe] had every right to due process and equal protection of the law."

Handicapped Infants Need Federal Protection

Nat Hentoff

Nat Hentoff is a well-known columnist for many liberal publications and a prominent civil libertarian who has published several articles opposing infant euthanasia. In the following viewpoint, Hentoff argues that when parents and doctors decide not to treat handicapped infants they discriminate against the infants. Frequently, the medical condition of handicapped infants can be greatly improved if corrective surgery is performed, Hentoff writes. Without such treatment, the handicap may become worse or may be deadly. He concludes that federal intervention is necessary to protect the handicapped newborns' right to life.

As you read, consider the following questions:

1. What point does Hentoff make by setting up the hypothetical example of a black infant who is denied medical treatment?
2. Why does the author disagree with the position taken by the American Civil Liberties Union?
3. What example does Hentoff cite to prove his contention that the media inaccurately reports "Infant Doe" cases? Why is this point important?

Nat Hentoff, "Is It Discriminatory To Kill Handicapped Infants?" *The Village Voice*, March 11, 1986. Reprinted with the author's permission.

[Doctors] call them bad babies. They didn't mean to be bad but who does.

from "The Ones That
Are Thrown Out," Miller Williams

Let us suppose a black infant is born with a deformed esophagus. Nothing else is wrong with him, but unless he has an operation to correct that deformity, he will not be able to eat as you and I do. He will have to be fed intravenously. The operation has a very high rate of success. The parents, however, do not wish the operation to take place. They are poor, unemployed, and believe that racism is so irreversibly endemic to America that they will not subject this child, who was not planned for to begin with, to a life of discrimination and its destructive effects.

Their physician respects the parents' view that if the infant were to survive, his "quality of life" might not be much. So the operation to fix the esophagus is not performed. Instructions are given the nurses that the infant is not to be fed intravenously. He is to be "allowed to die." That is, his parents and their physician are going to starve him to death. And they do.

Infanticide Is Being Practiced

What I have described has indeed happened, and quite often. Except for one thing. The infants who have been killed were dispatched not because of their race. They were sentenced to death because they were handicapped. For instance, infants with Down's syndrome have been starved to death in this manner. And some infants with spina bifida are "allowed to die." (Down's syndrome children are retarded, but it is impossible to tell at birth how retarded they will be. As for spina bifida children, when allowed to grow up, they're intelligent and involved members of the citizenry.)

If word got out that infanticide was being practiced solely on the basis that an infant was black, you'd hear about hardly anything else for weeks. The networks' news strips, *Nightline, Crossfire, Donahue, 60 Minutes,* a three-parter on *Like It Is,* and so on around the country. The producers' problem would be finding anyone supporting the view that black infants ought to be killed because they're black, no matter how racist this country is. And certainly every newspaper in the country would editorialize in horror at this ultimate form of discrimination, even if exercised by the parents themselves.

In real life, when word first got out—although this kind of killing had always been going on behind closed hospital doors—that an infant was eliminated solely because it was physically handicapped, there was an immediate furor. This was in 1982, when the parents of a Down's syndrome baby in Bloomington, Indiana, refused to permit an operation to repair his esophagus and the baby starved to death in six days. There were appalled editorials around the country, and appalled columnists.

Reaction to Federal Regulations

As news came, however, of more such cases of infanticide, the press, including the editorial writers, began to turn away from the dead babies because of a new development. In the wake of the Bloomington Baby, Ronald Reagan himself had been responsible for a set of hospital regulations intended to alert the Government to any future killings of handicapped infants. Doctors and editorial writers condemned these regulations as an intrusion by Big Brother into the time-honored private relationship between parents and physicians. The regulations were thrown out of court, others were substituted, and by then the starvation of the Bloomington Baby no longer seemed as shocking as the Government's invasion of the hospitals' and the parents' privacy.

Preventing Child Abuse

Ultimately, or ideally, the people are the government, and the handicapped child is a person—if you will, one of the people. Within that framework, can physicians, parents, or concerned citizens permit child abuse or deny the child certain rights? Can any one physician or family, whether out of conviction, ignorance or malice, in isolation or in a group, choose death over life for one of us? The need to safeguard the child from abuse, inadvertent or intentional, supersedes the right of the family to privacy. In cases of suspected abuse, concerned citizens have the right to know.

David G. McLone, *Issues in Law & Medicine*, July 1986.

Meanwhile, members of a new priesthood in the land, soft-voiced bioethicists, were telling David Brinkley, Ted Koppel, and the rest of us that there is no place for the rough hand of government in those terribly delicate moments during which only the parents have the right to decide what to do, and what not to do. And the American Civil Liberties Union heartily agreed. When the Federal Government wanted to get the hospital records of a spina bifida infant, Baby Jane Doe, on Long Island, the ACLU fiercely supported the right of the parents and the hospital to refuse the dictates of the insensitive Federal bureaucracy.

What the Government wanted to know, by the way, was the effect on the health of Baby Jane Doe of the parents' refusal to allow an immediate operation to repair the lesion in the spinal cord of the spina bifida child. That operation should be done very soon after birth or there is a strong likelihood of infection, and possibly permanent brain damage. Also, a shunt should have been inserted to drain the spinal fluid from the infant's brain; otherwise, the pressure on the brain can lead to mental retardation. The parents did not permit a shunt until months later.

Equal Protection of the Law

Everyone but the Government agreed, however, that the parents and their doctor should be left alone to do whatever they chose. Except for the right-to-lifers. They tried to intervene on behalf of the infant, but nobody took them seriously. Oh, there was one other exception. A number of disability rights groups supported the Government's attempt to obtain Baby Jane Doe's records. These are not right-to-lifers. But they know what it is to be disabled, so their concern was not solely for the parents. They remembered what everybody, including the press and the ACLU, forgot. They remembered Baby Jane Doe. She was not a fetus. She was *born*, and thereby had rights independent of her parents' wishes for her. As her own person under the Constitution, she had every right to due process and equal protection of the law. Both from a human rights and a Constitutional point of view, she should not have been denied the operation because she was handicapped.

Disability Rights Organizations

Oddly, with very few exceptions, the press, including television, did not mention the array of disability rights groups backing Baby Jane Doe in the Government's lawsuit to get her records. The strong impression given by the media was that only the right-to-lifers were cheering on Big Brother. Yet here is the list of organizations that were trying to ensure that Baby Jane Doe was not being discriminated against:

The American Coalition of Citizens with Disabilities, the Association for Retarded Citizens, the Association for the Severely Handicapped, the Disability Rights Education and Defense Fund, Disabled in Action of Metropolitan New York, and the Disability Rights Union.

So how was it possible that most people following the story had no idea that, in this case, the American Civil Liberties Union was vigorously opposing the most fundamental civil liberties of one spina bifida infant? The answer may be that there is something about the disabled, even when they are supported by organizations devoted to them, that causes the press, and most other people, to avert their eyes.

At the time, I talked with a number of members of disability rights organizations, and their interest in Baby Jane Doe's case was intense. As one of them, John Carlucci of Boston, a quadriplegic, said later, "We got into that fight because we knew that if society is not willing to assign a high value to a handicapped baby, then it will continue to have a low evaluation of the handicapped who *are* allowed into the world. If a Baby Doe doesn't have full rights, it's harder for us to get them."

As it turned out, the Second Circuit Court of Appeals decided, 2 to 1, that Baby Does don't have full rights. One of the rights they don't have is equal protection of the law. The Government had claimed that Section 504 of the Rehabilitation Act of 1973 surely applied to handicapped infants. That law says that no program receiving Federal assistance can discriminate against anyone who is handicapped. And the hospital where Baby Jane Doe was denied an operation to close the lesion on her spinal cord receives federal funds.

===

Federal Protection

A number of people said the government had no right to interfere in a matter that was the sole responsibility of the parents and the attending physicians. Yet there are truancy laws, child abuse laws, immunization laws, and so on, where the state's right to interfere is never seriously challenged. Those laws are accepted because, for the most part, they concern children who are no longer infants. . . .

[The Indiana] Baby Doe's life began with many tragic complications. But none of these handicaps put him outside the protection of the law. None of them relieved the state of its obligation to protect him. None of them permitted anyone to further jeopardize his health or his life.

C. Everett Koop, speech before the American Academy of Pediatrics' Committee of Hospital Care, September 19, 1984.

===

The majority of the three-judge Federal panel decided against the Government, saying that if Congress had wanted Section 504 to apply to Baby Does, it would have mentioned Baby Does in the language of the law. The language of 504 is broad is places, but it is hard to imagine, reading the legislation, that there was any way it could not have applied to handicapped infants. And that's the argument, made in dissent, by Judge Ralph Winter.

"A judgement not to perform certain surgery because a person is black is not a *bona fide* medical judgement. So, too, a decision not to correct a life-threatening digestive problem because an infant has Down's syndrome is not a *bona fide* medical judgement." Both decisions, Judge Winter said, are clearly discriminatory—the first because of race, the second because of disability. Section 504, therefore, obviously applies to the case of Baby Jane Doe.

Nonetheless, the case was dead—further evidence that when it comes to the disabled, judges, journalists, and the public at large do not see people with disabilities as fully belonging to this society.

The very language used by the able-bodied in talking about the less than able-bodied is slippery. Or, as Lisa Blumberg, a lawyer with cerebral palsy who writes about disability rights, says:

"Listen to the double talk. For most people, food is food, but for disabled infants, food suddenly became 'medical treatment' [which can be given or denied]. And 'severely handicapped' is a term that no one ever limits or defines." In nearly all the stories about Baby Jane Doe, it was as if her full name were severely-handicapped-Baby-Jane-Doe. Yet neither the reporters nor the editorial writers had any way of knowing the extent or degree of her handicaps because her hospital records had been sealed nine days after she was born, for fear of Big Brother getting at them. Months of this kind of "reporting" created the strong impression that the child was in such bad shape from the very beginning that nothing could have been done to improve her condition. All the more reason the parents ought to be left alone to deal with her as they thought best.

This self-fulfilling prophecy, so assiduously promoted by the press, influenced judges as well as the laity. One judge, who ruled on the case along the way, told me later he'd had no idea that it might have made a considerable difference if Baby Jane Doe had had the spinal cord operation as well as a shunt inserted very early on.

Misunderstanding the Issue

Oral arguments were heard in the United States Supreme Court on January 15, 1986, in a similar case dealing with whether Section 504 of the 1973 Rehabilitation Act can prevent hospitals from withholding treatment from handicapped infants. Disability rights lawyers who went to the oral arguments tell me they are not hopeful that the Supreme Court understands the issues.

Justice Byron White, for instance, expressed displeasure at the idea that the Federal Government would be "looking over the shoulders of doctors as to what standard [of medical treatment] they use."

Here is the specter of Big Brother again, conjured up so effectively by the ACLU in the Baby Jane Doe case in order to protect that infant. But from what? From medical treatment that might have inabled her to live a fuller life? The ACLU would not, I expect, spread fear of Big Brother if an infant were denied medical treatment by her parents only because she was black. The ACLU would roar for an immediate Federal presence in the hospital. . . .

Well, we're dealing only with what doctors call bad babies. Imperfect. Handicapped. What's wrong with killing them for their own good?

123

"The continuing attempt to enforce treatment by federal regulation is an ill-advised response to the problem of caring sensitively for severely compromised infants."

Federal Intervention Harms Infants' Interests

John C. Moskop and Rita L. Saldanha

Many health care professionals oppose federal attempts to intervene in treatment decisions regarding handicapped newborns. In the following viewpoint, John C. Moskop and Rita L. Saldanha argue against government intervention. The authors explain that current federal rules prohibit doctors from considering the child's future quality of life. In many cases, they conclude, these rules may in fact harm infants rather than protect them. Both authors are professors at the East Carolina University School of Medicine. Moskop teaches medical humanities and Saldanha teaches pediatrics/neonatology.

As you read, consider the following questions:

1. What are the three drawbacks to federal intervention cited by the authors?
2. What comparison do Moskop and Saldanha make regarding treatment decisions for adult patients and treatment decisions for infants?
3. According to the authors, in what situations does aggressively treating handicapped infants violate the Hippocratic Oath?

John C. Moskop and Rita L. Saldanha, "The Baby Doe Rule: Still a Threat," *Hastings Center Report*, April 1986. Reprinted with the authors' permission.

On April 15, 1985, the Department of Health and Human Services [DHHS] published a final rule entitled "Child Abuse and Neglect Prevention and Treatment Program," its fifth attempt in two years to formulate regulations regarding medical treatment of severely handicapped newborns. Like its predecessors, all of which were either struck down in the courts or revised in response to public comments, this latest "Baby Doe" rule has serious weaknesses.

The final regulations may indeed represent the best compromise achievable in the current political atmosphere. There remains, however, a major question: Should physicians feel confident that the new regulations will allow them to provide appropriate care for handicapped infants in all circumstances? We will argue that they should not.

The Rule's Intent

The intent of the current policy can be summarized in a single phrase from the rule: to prevent "the withholding of medically indicated treatment from a disabled infant with a life-threatening condition" by making such withholding an instance of medical neglect. The key term "withholding of medically indicated treatment" is further defined as " . . . the failure to respond to the infant's life-threatening conditions by providing treatment . . . which, in the treating physician's . . . reasonable medical judgment, will be most likely to be effective in ameliorating or correcting all such conditions." According to this policy, if there is a treatment that can ameliorate or correct an infant's life-threatening condition, that treatment must be provided.

Exceptions

The regulations go on to recognize three specific exceptions to this policy, that is, three circumstances in which treatment is not required. These exceptions are: (1) when "the infant is chronically and irreversibly comatose"; (2) when "treatment would merely prolong dying, not be effective in ameliorating or correcting all of the infant's life-threatening conditions, or otherwise be futile in terms of the survival of the infant"; and (3) when "treatment would be virtually futile in terms of the survival of the infant and the treatment itself under such circumstances would be inhumane.". . .

The goal of this policy, namely, to protect handicapped infants from medical neglect, is surely important, and the policy may result in long-term benefits for some infants who would otherwise have died for lack of treatment. Despite the highly publicized

Bloomington "Baby Doe" case, however, it is not clear that very many infants in recent years have been harmed by withholding or withdrawing medical care. In fact, largely *because* of widespread scholarly criticism of an earlier decision to withhold treatment from an infant with Down syndrome and duodenal atresia, the 1971 Johns Hopkins case, and a widely distributed film dramatization of this case called "Who Should Survive?" which was produced by the Joseph P. Kennedy, Jr. Foundation, such neglect probably occurred infrequently. In contrast to its 1983 warnings of widespread physician neglect of handicapped infants, DHHS now argues that its most recent regulations will affect the care of so few infants that no regulatory impact analysis is required.

The Right Decision

The Supreme Court was right to say that the delicate decisions about when and how to treat the Baby Does of this nation are better left to parents and physicians, operating against the background of state laws that protect all vulnerable people against homicide or medical neglect.

Alexander Morgan Capron, *Los Angeles Times*, June 15, 1986.

Thus, there may not have been a compelling need for new federal regulation in this area, especially since the current policy has at least three significant drawbacks. First, though it may prevent harm to some infants, the current policy threatens the significant harm of unjustified prolongation of life to other seriously handicapped infants. Second, because of the harm it would cause, the policy would force physicians to violate their traditional and fundamental obligation to do no harm without compensating benefit. Third, the policy may exacerbate existing problems or create new problems in the distribution of health care. These three problems will be examined in turn.

Significant Harms

Current federal policy threatens to create significant harms of unjustified prolongation of life to some seriously handicapped infants. In requiring that any infant whose life can be more than temporarily prolonged must be treated (provided that the infant is not irreversibly comatose), the policy comes close to supporting the principle of "vitalism"; namely, as Father John Paris describes it, that "life is the ultimate value, and something that is to be preserved regardless of prognosis, regardless of cost, and regardless of social considerations." The policy's only departures from this principle are its statements that infants who are permanently comatose, who are in the process of dying, or who are

126

highly unlikely to survive need not be treated.

The policy assumes, in other words, that noncomatose, nonterminal life is always preferable to nonexistence; it expressly prohibits consideration of the future quality of life of the infant. This, however, is not a plausible assumption; there are conditions other than irreversible coma or death in the near future in which people would overwhelmingly choose a shorter span of life over a longer life of a very poor quality. Treatment policies for adult patients recognize this possibility by requiring that physicians ordinarily obtain the informed consent of the patient even for life-saving or life-prolonging treatment.

An obvious difficulty in determining the value of life-prolonging care for infants is that infants cannot express preferences regarding the continuation of their lives; indeed, they do not have any such preferences. But this incapacity does not require that we doom some infants to longer lives of significant suffering. Where treatment has a high probability of causing significant pain and suffering and a low probability of preserving a life valuable to the patient, should we not permit a decision to withhold it?

The Role of Legal Guardians

In requiring that seriously handicapped infants be treated in almost all circumstances, the policy departs from a growing trend to allow legal guardians or next of kin in many circumstances to authorize the withholding or withdrawal of life-prolonging treatment that is not in the best interests of incompetent patients. The use of family contracts in extended care facilities and durable power of attorney designations for health care are examples of this trend.

Infants whose conditions are severe enough to raise questions about the wisdom of aggressive treatment are fairly common in neonatal intensive care units (NICUs). Among such conditions are extreme prematurity, severe intracranial hemorrhage, severe asphyxia, trisomy 13 and 18, and multiple severe congenital anomalies (such as high-lesion meningomyelocele with hydrocephalus, quadripligia, scoliosis, and incontinence). Sophisticated life-support systems make it possible to sustain the lives of infants with these conditions, at least for a time, but technology frequently cannot ameliorate the severe underlying handicaps. Neither do life support systems prevent life-threatening complications associated with prematurity, such as bronchopulmonary dysplasia (chronic lung disease), necrotizing enterocolitis (gangrene of the intestines), and severe intracranial hemorrhage.

In view of the suffering and uncertain prognosis of many of these infants, parents and health care professionals have found it extremely difficult to make decisions about withholding or withdrawing aggressive treatment. We recognize this difficulty and do not believe that a set of moral or technical criteria can be developed that would provide simple and clear solutions in all cases. We are concerned, however, that current federal policy significantly restricts the circumstances in which physicians and parents can act on their own considered judgments about what would be in the infant's best interests; instead it substitutes a hard and fast rule—whenever current technology can prolong life (that is, can prolong noncomatose life beyond the "near future"), it must be employed.

Duane C. Barnhart, for Greenhaven Press.

Admittedly, this policy greatly simplifies treatment decisions; parents and professionals need not, indeed may not, consider the "salvageable" infant's life prospects, no matter how harmful they may appear. A graphic illustration of the potential for harm in the treatment of a handicapped infant is provided by Robert and Peggy Stinson's account of their son Andrew, who was born on December 17, 1976 at a gestational age of 24½ weeks and a weight of 800 grams. He was placed on a respirator against his parents' wishes and without their consent on January 13, and remained dependent on the respirator until June 14, when he was finally permitted to die.

> The sad list of Andrew's afflictions, almost all of which were iatrogenic, reveals how disastrous this hospitalization was. Andrew had a months-long, unresolved case of bronchopulmonary dysplasia, sometimes referred to as "respirator lung syndrome." He was "saved" by the respirator to endure countless episodes of bradycardia and cyanosis, countless suctionings and tube insertions and blood samplings and blood transfusions, "saved" to develop retrolental fibroplasia, numerous infections, demineralized and fractured bones, an iatrogenic cleft palate, and, finally, as his lungs became irreparably diseased, pulmonary artery hypertension and seizures of the brain. He was, in effect "saved" by the respirator to die five long, painful, and expensive months later of the respirator's side effects.

We grant that this case may represent one of the worst treatment outcomes neonatologists could expect and that some of the elder Stinsons' problems may have been due to a poor relationship with their son's physicians. Nevertheless, as we understand the current policy, aggressive treatment of Andrew would be required until a judgment could be made that continued treatment was highly unlikely to prevent his death in the near future or that he was irreversibly comatose, that is, probably not before the last few weeks (or months) of his life. . . .

"Do No Harm"

If Mr. and Mrs. Stinson are correct in their judgment that aggressive treatment significantly harmed their son without the prospect of greater compensating benefits, then the physicians who treated him violated an ancient and honored Hippocratic principle of professional ethics, "Primum non nocere," "First, do no harm." In an era in which powerful treatments often produce significant harms as well as benefits, this principle requires interpretation. One obvious interpretation is that, absent special circumstances such as a patient's specific request, treatments that promise greater overall harm than benefit to the patient ought not be provided. As already noted, determining when prolonging treatment constitutes a harm to the patient is not a simple matter, but

129

neither is it impossible or purely arbitrary. At some point, the harms of painful and disabling treatment must surely outweigh the benefit of some chance at survival with a much diminished quality of life. At that point, providing further treatment violates the physician's commitment to do no harm. . . .

Diminished Quality of Life

There comes a point at which further prolongation of one's life simply does not make up for the burden of continued aggressive treatment, especially if the quality of life prolonged is diminished by suffering and incapacity. If it would be cruel to prolong the life of adult patients under these circumstances, then it must also be cruel to prolong the life of handicapped infants under comparable circumstances. . . .

Finally, as a high-technology, labor-intensive area of medical care, neonatal intensive care is both very expensive and in relatively short supply. By requiring treatment under almost all circumstances, the Baby Doe rule will likely add to the supply problem. NICUs will have to devote a larger proportion of their beds to the most severely and chronically disabled infants, infants like Andrew Stinson who will have very lengthy stays in intensive care, some with limited prospects of ever leaving the unit. As this occurs it will become more and more difficult to provide intensive care promptly for all those infants with acute but completely reversible life-threatening conditions. Such infants may need to be tranported long distances to secure care; occasionally their condition may deteriorate or they may die while they are waiting for a bed to become available.

For all the above reasons, the threat of unjustified prolongation of life, the violation of the physician's duty to do no harm, and undesirable effects on the distribution of health care, the continuing attempt to enforce treatment by federal regulation is an ill-advised response to the problem of caring sensitively for severely compromised infants. We should be proud that our health care system is able to care for very sick newborns, but also recognize that there are limits to our powers. In medicine as elsewhere, advanced technology cannot cure all the ills to which we are heir. And, as the power of any technology increases, so does its potential for harm.

Distinguishing Between Fact and Opinion

This activity is designed to help develop the basic reading and thinking skill of distinguishing between fact and opinion. Consider the following statement as an example: "Baby Doe in Indiana died within a week after his Down's Syndrome went untreated." This is a fact—the baby in Indiana did die after not being treated. But the statement "Baby Doe could have lived a long, rich life had his doctors and parents decided to treat him," is an opinion. No one knows for sure what sort of life Baby Doe would have lived. There is no way to prove whether this statement is true or false.

When investigating controversial issues it is important that one be able to distinguish between statements of fact and statements of opinion. It is also important to recognize that not all statements of fact are true. They may appear to be true, but some are based on inaccurate or false information. For this activity, however, we are concerned with understanding the difference between those statements which appear to be factual and those which appear to be based primarily on opinion.

Most of the following statements are taken from the viewpoints in this chapter. Consider each statement carefully. *Mark O for any statement you believe is an opinion or interpretation of facts. Mark F for any statement you believe is a fact. Mark I for any statement you believe is impossible to judge.*

If you are doing this activity as a member of a class or group, compare your answers with those of other class or group members. Be able to defend your answers. You may discover that others come to different conclusions than you do. Listening to the reasons others present for their answers may give you valuable insights in distinguishing between fact and opinion.

If you are reading this book alone, ask others if they agree with your answers. You too will find this interaction valuable.

O = *opinion*
F = *fact*
I = *impossible to judge*

131

1. On April 9, 1982, a baby boy known only as Baby Doe was born in a hospital in Bloomington, Indiana.

2. Current federal policy threatens to harm handicapped infants by requiring that their lives be unjustifiably prolonged.

3. The killing of a human being is not of unique moral significance.

4. According to a national poll, three-fourths of the nation's pediatric surgeons would refuse a life-saving operation for a handicapped child.

5. So-called right to life organizations step into a life, do their thing, clap their hands, and after it's done they turn away.

6. Decisions involving the care of hopelessly ill newborns should be left to parents and doctors.

7. Taxpayers are paying well over $43,000 a year to maintain the life of Cara Bailey.

8. Baby Jane Doe was severely handicapped.

9. When it comes to the disabled, judges, journalists, and the public at large do not see people with disabilities as fully belonging to this society.

10. Plato's *Republic* advocates killing defective newborns.

11. The death of our handicapped babies moves us several steps further down the slippery slope of planned death for all those who don't measure up to our standards of what it means to be a person.

12. Infanticide threatens none of us who are rational, self-aware humans, for once we are aware of it, we are not infants.

13. Baby Doe's parents refused to consent to surgery for their child.

14. Not every decision to withhold or withdraw treatment from a critically ill child is infanticide.

15. Pigs, cows, and chickens have a greater capacity to relate to others, better ability to communicate, and far more curiosity, than the most severely retarded humans.

Periodical Bibliography

The following list of periodical articles deals with the subject matter of this chapter.

America   "If Not That Way, What Way?" July 26, 1986.

George J. Annas   "Checkmating the Baby Doe Regulations," *Hastings Center Report,* August 1986.

Steven Baer   "Should Imperfect Infants Survive?" *National Review,* September 2, 1983.

Raymond S. Duff and A.G.M. Campbell   "Moral and Ethical Dilemmas in the Special Care Nursery," *The New England Journal of Medicine,* October 25, 1973.

Nat Hentoff   "Nat Hentoff on the Babies Doe," *The Human Life Review,* Spring 1984.

Ruth Hubbard   "Caring for Baby Doe," *Ms.,* May 1984.

Andrew H. Malcolm   "Fate of 20-Ounce Baby Is Test of Medical Ethics," *The New York Times,* November 13, 1984.

The National Review   "Baby Jane Doe," February 10, 1984.

John J. Paris   "Right to Life Doesn't Demand Heroic Sacrifice," *The Wall Street Journal,* November 28, 1983.

Nancy K. Rhoden   "Treating Baby Doe: The Ethics of Uncertainty," *Hastings Center Report,* August 1986.

Carlton Sherwood   "US Officials Ignore Disabled Babies' Plight," *The Washington Times,* July 9, 1984.

Susan Talbot   "Nathan: A Family's Experience with Infanticide," *National Right to Life News,* December 19, 1985.

Mary Tedeschi   "Infanticide & Its Apologists," *Commentary,* November 1984.

U.S. News & World Report   "Pro and Con: Should Uncle Sam Protect Handicapped Babies?" January 16, 1984.

Mary Warnock   "The Right to Death," *The New Republic,* February 17, 1986.

Should Euthanasia
Be Allowed?

**death
and dying**

"A quick and merciful end should be a medical option."

Euthanasia Is Justified

Larry Larson and Alan L. Otten

Many proponents of euthanasia believe the quality of human life is more important than the length of life. In the following viewpoint, Larry Larson and Alan L. Otten explain why they believe euthanasia should be public policy. Larson is a hospital health-unit coordinator in Minneapolis and Otten is a senior national correspondent for *The Wall Street Journal*. In Part I Larson argues that people facing lengthy, dehumanizing deaths should be able to decide when and how they will die. Otten in Part II describes the horrible pain his 90-year-old, bed-ridden mother suffers in a nursing home. For some people, he concludes, legal euthanasia would be the most humane choice.

As you read, consider the following questions:

1. What point do the authors make by discussing how society treats dying animals?
2. What position is truly "pro-life," according to Larson?
3. What is Otten's suggestion for making decisions on euthanasia cases?

Larry Larson, "Legal, Active Euthanasia Should Be an Option for Patients Facing Death," *Minneapolis Star and Tribune*, June 1, 1985. Reprinted by permission of the Minneapolis Star and Tribune.

Alan L. Otten, "Can't We Put My Mother to Sleep?" *The Wall Street Journal*, June 5, 1985. Reprinted by permission of *The Wall Street Journal*, © Dow Jones & Company, Inc. 1985. All Rights Reserved.

I

In America we perform abortions, execute murderers and draft young men so they may be slain for their country. But mention the subject of euthanasia and people start to get a little crazy.

Having worked in a variety of medical settings, I have seen countless people suffer hideous deaths from illnesses like cancer, AIDS, cirrhosis and end-stage pulmonary disease. A dying animal is quickly "put out of its misery," but no such consideration is offered the terminally ill human.

Where there is life there may be hope. But where there is life there is also inevitable death. Doctors often act as if death were just another health problem that could be cured with enough effort. Perhaps it is time our society and its grandiose medical profession relieved themselves of the myth of immortality.

The Need for Legislation

Passive euthanasia, which allows people to die without heroic, life-sustaining, death-prolonging efforts, is already being practiced in the United States. But active euthanasia seems a long way off. In The Netherlands, the terminally ill may request and legally receive life-terminating drugs. It is time the United States passed legislation to allow similar treatment for the dying.

While no one should have active euthanasia forced on them, neither should it be denied to those who might request it. For those who have entered the dark and hopeless world of metastatic cancer, full-blown AIDS or progressive Alzheimer's, a quick and merciful end should be a medical option.

Dr. Christiaan Barnard, the first to transplant a human heart, talked on this subject at the 1984 World Euthanasia Conference in Nice, France. He said he had practiced passive euthanasia and would practice active euthanasia if not for the legal ramifications. Barnard said, "I believe often that death is good medical treatment because it can achieve what all the medical advances and technology cannot achieve today, and that is stop the suffering of the patient."

Death's Inevitability

A truly prolife stance recognizes the inevitability of death and the wisdom of sparing the terminally ill a dying process that destroys the body, mind and very sense of self.

In 1935, feminist Frances Perkins Gilman, a supporter of legal euthanasia, took her own life. She was dying of cancer. She left a manuscript explaining that "the record of a previously noble life is precisely what makes it sheer insult to allow death in pitiful

136

degradation. We may not wish to 'die with our boots on' but we may well prefer to die with our brains on . . . I have preferred chloroform to cancer."

Currently, euthanasia is an unpopular idea. I suspect it will become more acceptable as time goes on. The cost of treating America's AIDS victims is estimated already to be several billion dollars, and the epidemic has only begun. Even more awesome to contemplate is the growing population of illness-prone, elderly Americans. If Medicare cuts are being proposed now, what does the future hold? Economic necessity, not humanitarian concern, may require euthanasia. It is unfortunate that we will be doing the right thing for the wrong reason.

II

When I was a boy, my family had a beloved bulldog. Eventually he became very old—blind, incontinent, wheezing heavily, barely able to eat or walk. We took him to the vet and, as the euphemism then had it, the vet "put Jerry to sleep."

Every few days now, I go to visit my 90-year-old mother in a nearby nursing home, more to salve my own conscience probably than to do her any meaningful service. For her, in fact, there is little I can do. She lies on her side in bed, legs drawn rigidly into a fetal position, blinks at me uncomprehendingly as I prattle on about family doings, and rarely utters a sound except a shriek of

'Happy birthday, Dear Mr. Trumbull, happy birthday to youuuuuuuu!'

Wayne Stayskal. Reprinted by permission: Tribune Media Services.

pain when the attendants turn her from one side to the other in their constant battle to heal her horrible bedsores. She must be hand-fed, and her incontinency requires a urethral catheter.

Why do we treat our aged and loved animals better than we treat our aged and loved human beings? Shouldn't a humane, caring society—as ours is supposed to be—begin to consider ways to put my long-suffering mother, and the steadily growing number of miserable others like her, peacefully to sleep?

Empty Lives

My mother is far from a unique case now, and as our society continues to age, there'll be more and more like her—very old people, enduring barren year after barren year, with chronic diseases that unfortunately do not kill but merely irrevocably waste the body and destroy the mind.

Doctors, nursing homes and hospitals work to keep these old people alive with tube feeding, nutritional supplements, antibiotics at the first sign of infection. For what? Are we really doing these people any favor by fighting so hard to prolong their lives?

I am not talking about physically impaired old people who may still be mentally alert, or those whose minds are, as the young people say, out to lunch but who are still comparatively fit physically. I am talking about the many thousands of old men and women disastrously and hopelessly crippled both in mind and body. Does it really make sense to keep extending lives that are so empty of even an occasional moment of recognition or joy— unable to know a loved grandchild, savor a long-favorite food, carry on even the simplest conversation?

As the Rev. John Paris, a Jesuit priest who teaches ethics at Holy Cross College, says: "In our determination to prolong life at any cost, we have forgotten that dying is part of the process of living. These people's bodies are telling them there really is no purpose in going on, and yet we make them go on."

Hard-Won Progress

Of late, there seems to be a growing though reluctant recognition that a mentally competent person who is terminally ill or in extreme pain should be able to refuse respirators or other life-lengthening measures. Even more reluctantly, some states are accepting the next of kin's right to make such a decision for a terminally ill but mentally incompetent patient.

Yet this hard-won progress doesn't help the growing numbers like my mother. Heart and lungs are working, whatever is wrong with spine and limbs and mind. There is no respirator to be unplugged. No doctor can pronounce her a terminal case. The only sure prognosis is constant pain and misery as long as she lives.

Over and over, healthy middle-aged people today voice their dread of ending their days in this vegetative state. Over and over, ailing old men and women wail, "Why is God punishing me this way? Why can't I die?"

The Patient's Best Interest

Euthanasia has tended to be a dirty word in this country, but isn't it time to respond to these *cris de coeur*? American medicine is supposed to operate in the best interest of the patient; prolonging a life of incurable wretchedness turns that standard upside down.

The euthanasia slope is, of course, slippery, but that doesn't make descent impossible. We just must walk extra carefully.

Doctors and medical ethicists surely should be able to work out the best possible techniques for making so sensitive a decision, hedging them around with special safeguards. Many hospitals use ethics committees to set guidelines for withdrawing life-support systems from the terminally ill. Couldn't these committees similarly set rules for deciding when and how to withdraw life from elderly men and women whose minds and bodies are tragically wrecked beyond repair?

Like a Vegetable

"I am 82 years old," Harriet E. Shulan told the medical team in her hospital room in Phoenix, Arizona, "and I don't want this done."

Nonetheless, the life-sustaining tubes were inserted up her nose and down her throat and into her arms. "Annabelle," the patient cried as her daughter entered the room, "how can you do this to me? Don't let me live like a vegetable!" . . .

On several visits, Mrs. Shulan took her daughter's hand and tried to get her to unfasten the tubes. Mrs. Lurie explained that she could not do that. And then her mother, Mrs. Lurie tearfully remembers now, "withdrew into a little world of her own, because life was just too intolerable." . . .

A tearful Mrs. Lurie said, "Mother had a good life. I'm not crying about her death, but for the way she had to go."

Andrew H. Malcolm, *International Herald Tribune,* October 3, 1984.

Many doctors say they would be prepared, at a minimum, to let nature take its course as these people deteriorate—forgoing the tube feeding, antibiotics and other delaying mechanisms. That would at least bring natural death a little sooner. And actually, several doctors tell me, this approach is already being used more often than society realizes.

A futher step would be to withhold food and water; debate over the wisdom and ethics of this is already under way among lawyers, doctors and ethicists. The New Jersey Supreme Court, in a recent trailblazing decision, held that food and water could be withdrawn to hasten a dying person's end if that was clearly what the person wished or would have wished.

Interestingly, when I told several doctors and ethicists about my mother, they all offered the same suggestion: Take her home, keep her comfortable, moisten her lips and bathe off her body from time to time, but nothing more. In essence, just hold her hand and help her through the dying.

Quick and Humane

But why must it be done this slow, hard way? Why not a pill, injection or other quick and more humane method, once the doctors' committee or other decision-making panel has agreed there's no point in making the elderly person suffer any longer?

Clearly, opposition to this entire proposal will be intense. In the recent Baby Doe controversy, the administration and Congress rushed to mandate the continuation of life, however dismal, and presumably the same response awaits the first case of Old Lady Doe.

Yet the public may be readier to move than many leaders think. Opinion polls show overwhelming—and steadily rising—support for the idea of allowing terminally ill patients to die quickly. A recent Harris Poll, for example, found 85% now, as against 62% in 1973, endorsing a terminally ill patient's right to tell the doctor to stop trying to extend life, and 61% now (as against only 37% in 1973) favoring the patient's right to ask the doctor actually to "put him out of his misery."

True, these questions involve the terminally ill, yet the remarkably high percentages can't help but indicate substantial, though admittedly smaller, support for similar treatment of the hopelessly vegetative.

The Quality of Life

"We need to educate people to the idea that the quality of life is more important than mere length of life," argues University of Virginia ethicist Joseph Fletcher. "Our cultural tradition holds that life has absolute value, but that's really not good enough any more. Sometimes, no life may be better."

I'm sure that if my mother could think and speak, she would agree.

"*Although it is tempting to take an absolute stand against active euthanasia, the recognition of tragic, exceptional circumstances makes it impossible for me to do so.*"

Euthanasia Is Sometimes Justified

Lowell O. Erdahl

Lowell O. Erdahl is an author and the bishop of the Southeastern Minnesota District of the American Lutheran Church. In the following viewpoint, he argues that euthanasia may be acceptable in a few, specific cases. Erdahl opposes institutionalized euthanasia because he believes it could lead to serious abuses and would reduce the value society places on human life. Yet, he concludes, a pro-life position must recognize that in some tragic situations euthanasia is the only answer.

As you read, consider the following questions:

1. Why does the author oppose institutionalized euthanasia?
2. What is the difference between active and passive euthanasia, according to Erdahl?
3. What pro-life alternative to euthanasia does the author suggest?

Reprinted by permission from PRO-LIFE/PRO-PEACE by Lowell O. Erdahl, copyright © 1986 Augsburg Publishing House.

INTRO

Doctors, families, and patients themselves now face many choices that were not available to previous generations. The use of "artificial" life-support systems inevitably leads to situations that require choices concerning the rightness or wrongness of "pulling the plug" and raises as never before the issue of mercy killing or *euthanasia,* which literally means "good death."

These changes, however, did not create the problem. . . . The possibility of deliberately ending the life of a suffering person has always been present. We note that in at least two ways medical advances make consideration of mercy killing less pressing than in times past. One is that many formerly devastating illnesses and conditions of distressing disability can now be cured, corrected, or managed so that meaningful life is now possible. The other is that painkilling drugs eliminate much of the intense suffering formerly experienced by millions. The prospect of such suffering moved Mahatma Gandhi, who lived with great reverence for life and opposition to violence, to contemplate the possibility of being required by love and sacred duty to take the life of his own child as the only means of relieving the anguish of incurable rabies. We thank God that the comforts of modern medicine now offer alternatives for the relief of such suffering.

Difficult Cases

On the other hand, the ability to maintain biological functions that would have otherwise ceased has brought the question of euthanasia into sharper focus. The difficult cases are not those in which brain death has already occurred. When the brain is dead, the person has died. There is, therefore, no justification for maintaining the biological functions, except temporarily in order to preserve organs for transplant. The agonizing cases are those in which the person remains alive but with little, if any, prospect of healing and meaningful life.

The pro-life perspective—which grants that there are tragic exceptional circumstances when the taking of life is justifiable, but which opposes all forms of institutionalized and established killing—also applies to mercy killing. That is, passive or even active euthanasia may sometimes be justifiable in a specific situation, but it is wrong when institutionalized in accepted practice, as, for example, under Hitler in the Nazi era. . . .

Although passive euthanasia is widely accepted, there are strong emotional and legal barriers to active euthanasia. Doctors are permitted to refrain from treatments that would prolong their patients' lives, but are not allowed to administer drugs to kill them. Is such a distinction between passive and active euthanasia always morally justifiable? Are there circumstances in which it is right to practice active euthanasia?

Although it is tempting to take an absolute stand against active euthanasia, the recognition of tragic, exceptional circumstances makes it impossible for me to do so. Just as there are situations in which it may be justifiable to kill the unborn, the enemy warrior, or the criminal intent on murder, there may be also circumstances in which active euthanasia is more compassionate than passive. Is it, for example, more kind to cause death by dehydration and starvation than it is to kill the patient by lethal injection? In both cases the motive and effect are exactly the same; only the method is different. Is it possible that in some cases the sin of omission (permitting death by dehydration and starvation) may be greater than the sin of commission (causing death by lethal injection)?

Emotionally it is obviously much easier for the family and doctor to permit the patient to die than to deliberately kill the patient. But is there a similar logical and moral difference? Raising such a question reminds us of the extent to which emotion, rather

than logical or moral considerations, often prevails in life and death decisions. Many people, for example, are appalled at the thought of deliberately killing their 95-year-old grandmother who has been in a coma for months and for whom there is no prospect of meaningful life; but at the same time they are advocates of abortion on demand. Is it not, however, more moral to deliberately act to end life's final suffering than to foreclose the possibility of life fulfillment at its beginning? The point of this observation is not to affirm active euthanasia (to me it is more of an argument against easy abortion), but to underscore the emotional rather than ethical basis of many of our decisions.

Risking the Slippery Slope

While granting that it may be morally justifiable in exceptional circumstances, I see great danger in the cultural and legal acceptance of active euthanasia. Taking this step places our feet on a slippery slope on which we can quickly slide into easy and irreverent mercy killing for unjustifiable reasons and then on into the institutionalized and established practice of euthanasia for economic and social purposes, as practiced by Hitler. If laws are changed to permit active euthanasia in rare, justifiable circumstances, it will require extreme vigilance to prevent these exceptions from becoming standard practice.

It is reported that the average age of nursing-home residents is now 83 and rising. Medical costs continue to escalate, in spite of efforts to contain them. Some speak of the responsibility of the elderly to die in order to ease the burden on the younger generation. These signs of our times tell of increasing pressure for public acceptance of active as well as passive euthanasia. They are small steps down a road that could lead to provisions for the permitted, and possibly even required, elimination not only of the suffering, senile, and elderly, but also of others of all ages who have been determined to be nonproductive members of society. Therefore, even though there may be exceptional circumstances in which active euthanasia is justified, I believe that it is wiser public policy to continue to prohibit it altogether rather than risk the temptations and tendencies of this slippery slope.

In summary, passive euthanasia may be justifiable (1) when it is determined that the patient is irreversibly comatose, (2) when the treatment prolongs imminent and inevitable death, and (3) when the treatment itself is so traumatic that it is inhumane to administer it. In addition to these criteria, active euthanasia should never be permitted or even considered unless it is clearly inhumane to let an illness run its course and there is no other means of ending meaningless suffering. . . .

The pro-life alternatives to euthanasia include everything possible to provide compassionate and often costly care of the ill, infirm, and elderly. The true test of a society's faithfulness to the pro-life perspective is not only in its opposition to killing but also in its willingness to make adequate provision for those who are suffering and nonproductive. As costs of care increase, individuals in specific circumstances and society as a whole will be strongly tempted to sell out both compassion and responsible reverence for life in exchange for economic considerations. If the day comes when euthanasia is established as an economic policy, we will have ceased to be either fully moral or fully human. It is imperative that we oppose every step toward irresponsible euthanasia and also affirm the reordering of the priorities and expenditures of our personal and corporate life in order to provide the compassionate care every human being deserves. If we are not vigilant in opposition to unjustifiable euthanasia, we may one day be haunted by horrors more antiseptic, but no less terrifying, than Hitler's "final solution."

"Legalized euthanasia would . . . create a whole class of admittedly human persons who are subject to death."

Euthanasia Is Never Justified

Frank Morriss

Many opponents to euthanasia believe the term is a euphemism for murder. Right-to-life groups believe that when euthanasia becomes sanctioned by the state, other barriers against killing will fall. In the following viewpoint, Frank Morriss writes that the state must defend the right to life as the basis for a safe society. Morriss, a contributing editor for *The Wanderer*, a conservative Catholic newspaper, also disputes the argument for "mercy killing." Should euthanasia become legal, he argues, those citizens considered burdensome and disposable would be at great risk.

As you read, consider the following questions:

1. According to the author, why should the state not be given sovereignty over life, even for "good motives"?
2. What danger does Morriss see in the state allowing "mercy killing"?
3. Morriss argues that individuals should not be allowed to evaluate life's worth. Why?

Frank Morriss, "Euthanasia—No!" a position paper, November 3, 1986. Reprinted with the author's permission.

What I am insisting must not be done is to legalize murder or suicide for the motive of mercy. Consider what that would amount to. It would for the first time in the history of Western civilization and jurisprudence deliver to individuals sovereignty over innocent life—either someone else's life or one's own. This would be an historic reversal of the concept that no one, not individual or state or any person, is the absolute master of life, life being the highest and most fundamental good and the basic right. Not even in legalized abortion has such a claim been made; even here there has been recognized the need of holding to the idea (whether as fiction or fact) that what is killed in the womb is not a person, not an individual human life.

Legalized euthanasia, however, would discard such pretense and create a whole class of admittedly human persons who are subject to death, though innocent of any crime and certainly in no way aggressors or enemies of society. Conceding for the moment and only for the point of discussion that under such a law some acts of ending great pain might occur. Still, the precedent and idea that innocent life is dispensable, though for supposed "good" motive, would have put the whole common good in danger. Once the state, through law, has conceded sovereignty over life for one motive, there is no reason that any motive the state judges desirable should not be the excuse for legally disposing of innocent life. With legalized euthanasia we have entered the Hitlerian nightmare, or the Orwellian prophecy of the subjection of the individual to the omnipotent state.

Surely sovereignty over life is the mark of omnipotence. To claim it is to set up a type of idolatry. Since Greek recognition of the natural law, Western civilization has seen the necessity of leaving sovereignty over life to true Omnipotence, to the Creator of life. The alternative is to make the state a kind of life-devouring Moloch. It does not change that reality by insisting that euthanasia is a kind act of a benign society or government. The nature of what would be done by legalizing euthanasia is not changed even were that argument to be granted. A state holding sovereignty over innocent life is a monstrous usurper, whether benign or not.

"Mercy" as a Motive

Let us turn to more practical aspects of this question. Under legalized euthanasia the presumption of innocence on the part of the one taking the life surely would be established. One need only plead "mercy" as motive to invoke the protection of the law. This puts those who consider themselves burdened by guardianship of the elderly or the suffering at a distinct advantage. How dif-

"I KNEW I SHOULD HAVE ABORTED YOU LIKE ALL THE REST, LEON!"

Wayne Stayskal. Reprinted by permission: Tribune Media Services.

ficult it would be to question the plea of mercy on the part of anyone who could summon up a tear or two, when the real motive might have been to get out from under a burden, or more crass, perhaps to come into an inheritance. If the quality of mercy is not strained, it is also very difficult to genuinely establish—or to deny. It is hidden in the depths of the human heart and conscience, and there it should remain, not enthroned and made ruler over life by legal fiat.

The inalienability of life is in fact the concern of the state, for that inalienability is the basis for a safe society in which the natural law—the law dictated by man's true nature and true purpose—prevails. This applies even when it is a question of suicide, so that such an act has for all of Western civilization been outlawed, and still is in most jurisdictions.

Suicide and Euthanasia

But, you say, surely individuals should be able to end or have ended their own lives when suffering and pain become unendurable. But if that is to be so you have made each individual the evaluator of the worth of life. Under the evil influence of some philosophers, life has at times been held undesirable under any circumstances. The medieval Cathars and pure ones of the Albigensian heresy taught the worthlessness—even evil—of life. Suicide was considered the highest act of virtue. Can the state surrender to such a despairing philosophy? . . .

148

Suicide is a major problem with young persons today. Legalized euthanasia would simply tell them it is not a problem—but their right. Who can set limits to the claim to "mercy" as a motive for suicide, once the idea is accepted and legalized? Despair and pessimism will in effect have been canonized by law.

Disposable People

Euthanasia concerns the type of society we wish to live in and bequeath to our children. Established as right, proper, and legal, euthanasia would be part of a society where all life is subject to state determination. Equal protection of the laws for any class of people the state considered disposable would be meaningless. Mercy for the suffering or elderly could next be "mercy" for the deformed, the defective, the burdensome. Those of differing values and philosophies could then be the subjects of state recognized "mercy."

No horror against life is impossible once we have allowed anyone but the Creator to usurp sovereignty over life. Whom the gods would destroy they first make mad. Legalized euthanasia is such madness.

"You have the right to refuse cruel, costly, life-prolonging treatment."

Living Wills Are Necessary

A.J. Levinson and Jacob K. Javits

The "living will" has become a popular document within the right-to-die movement. Signers of the living will ask that doctors not continue extraordinary medical treatment should they become incapacitated and terminally ill. Part I of the following viewpoint is written by A.J. Levinson, executive director of Concern for Dying, a right-to-die interest group. Levinson presents a brief overview of the need for a living will. In Part II, Jacob K. Javits, a former senator from New York, writes that people with terminal illnesses should be allowed to die with dignity through the use of living wills. Javits, who suffered from Lou Gehrig's disease, died six months after writing this viewpoint.

As you read, consider the following questions:

1. Why does Levinson suggest that people should make out living wills?
2. According to Javits, why should everyone be concerned about the "right to die"?
3. What is Javits' main reason for advocating the use of living wills?

A.J. Levinson, "Avoid Anguish With a Living Will," USA TODAY, January 11, 1985.
Copyright, 1986 USA TODAY. Reprinted with permission.
Jacob K. Javits, "Life, Death and Human Dignity," The New York Times, August 18, 1985.
Copyright © 1985 by The New York Times Company. Reprinted by permission.

I

Y ou have the right to refuse cruel, costly, life-prolonging treatment. Legal experts agree that the choice is yours.

Yet you, like William Bartling [a terminally ill man kept alive by life support systems for seven months], may be in danger of having your rights ignored. Your family, like the Bartlings, could be forced to endure increased emotional suffering and financial strains as you are forced to linger near death.

What explains this contradiction?

The answer is painfully simple: Unless everyone involved in the decision to withhold or withdraw life-sustaining treatment knows about your exact wishes, the result can be confusion and uncertainty.

To make sure your death is not unnecessarily prolonged, you must decide how you feel about various methods of treatment and convey your thoughts in writing to others. Otherwise, the possibility of a court case is all too real.

The Need for a Living Will

Concern For Dying developed the living will to prevent legal obscenities like the Bartling case and to make it easier to deal with this difficult subject. With this document, you can specify before being incapacitated your wishes regarding the use of life-sustaining treatment when death is imminent and designate a person to make decisions if you cannot.

There is a variety of forms available for this purpose: Living wills, directives specified by 22 states, and durable powers of attorney. All of the specificity in the world, however, will have no effect if no one knows your feelings.

After preparing a living will, it is imperative that you give copies to your family, physician, religious adviser, and anyone else who may be involved in decision-making at the end of your life. This can serve as material proof of your convictions.

Finally, you can turn to Concern for Dying if a Living Will is not being honored. We have helped to resolve hundreds of cases, such as a recent one in which a woman had been kept on life support for several months though blind, paralyzed, irreversibly comatose, and a double amputee. Concern for Dying provided the expertise and legal counsel necessary to end the unwanted and unwarranted treatment.

Do what you can to spare yourself and your family the anguish and expense of prolonged medical intervention and/or legal action when you are dying.

To My Family, My Physician, My Lawyer and All Others Whom It May Concern

Death is as much a reality as birth, growth, maturity and old age—it is the one certainty of life. If the time comes when I can no longer take part in decisions for my own future, let this statement stand as an expression of my wishes and directions, while I am still of sound mind.

If at such a time the situation should arise in which there is no reasonable expectation of my recovery from extreme physical or mental disability, I direct that I be allowed to die and not be kept alive by medications, artificial means or "heroic measures". I do, however, ask that medication be mercifully administered to me to alleviate suffering even though this may shorten my remaining life.

This statement is made after careful consideration and is in accordance with my strong convictions and beliefs. I want the wishes and directions here expressed carried out to the extent permitted by law. Insofar as they are not legally enforceable, I hope that those to whom this Will is addressed will regard themselves as morally bound by these provisions.

Signed _____

Date _____

Witness _____

Witness _____

Copies of this request have been given to _____

_____

_____

Frank Harron, John Burnside, Tom Beauchamp, eds., *Health and Human Values*. New Haven, CT: Yale University Press, 1983. Copyright © by Yale University.

II

I may be terminally ill. I therefore face, in an intimate and personal way, the issue of my right to die. I am happy for those who are not ill, but they are terminal too and they should think about this question as it relates to themselves and those they love as friends or family or simply fellow human beings.

The issue first received serious attention 10 years ago, when a

New Jersey court granted Karen Ann Quinlan's parents' request to remove life-preserving support from their comatose daughter. There has, since then, been an intensive inquiry into the ethical and legal aspects of the right to die.

The issue is whether a terminally ill patient may confer the authority to withdraw his life support. This is generally done by means of a living will, written when the patient is still competent, that transfers authority to a designated relative, friend, physician, religious or legal adviser or to a court. Thirty-five states have now passed living-will laws, 22 of them in the last decade.

Ability To Decide

The question arises in the case of any serious illness—including cancer, heart attack and a whole range of neurological and neuromuscular diseases—that deprives the patient of the ability to decide what is to be done for him. But once illness has struck, it is often too late: the patient is often no longer competent to express a will.

Birth and death are the most singular events we experience— and the contemplation of death, as of birth, should be a thing of beauty, not ignobility. Everyone must think about dying, young and old alike, though older people are at greater risk. Given the new medical technology that can sustain life even when the brain is gone, we must also think about the right to die and the need for dignity in departing life.

Happily, my mind is still functioning, but if it should stop, I believe, I would be dead—and there would be no use in prolonging the agony. We owe it to ourselves and the ones we love to make provision for such moments. It is in the highest interest of humanitarianism that we prepare for these moments with living-will laws. . . .

Legal Death

From a legal point of view, living wills are no different from wills that leave property, appoint guardians for children and establish trusts for charity, education and research. As lawyers help people make such ordinary wills, so they should help people provide for their living and dying. The individual making the will must be of sound mind and have the capacity to express his own wishes as to the disposition of his body. These wills could also provide for the contribution, for use in transplants, of bodily organs that are no longer of any use to the individual. Lawyers should have that responsibility, too.

The authority conferred by a living will must not, of course, be abused. Nothing could be more important, after all, than the right to life—and the right not to have it terminated prematurely. In the event of flagrant abuse, or any possibility of it—when a decision may seem to defy the wishes of the individual who made the will, or when loved ones are unable to determine if it should be invoked,—then, of course, the patient's relatives must have recourse to the courts.

Dignity in Death

The issue of living wills is under consideration now by the American Bar Association, the American Medical Association, the Pacific Presbyterian Medical Center of San Francisco and the Committees on the Aging in both the Senate and the House of Representatives, among other organizations. We can only hope that they will all understand the need to preserve the dignity that is most precious to an older person or anyone else who has to think imminently about dying. Surely that dignity is best served by avoiding the confusion that comes from not having a will about mortality.

Short of a living will, the best way to provide that dignity is to use the durable power of attorney to appoint an individual to make medical decisions when the patient concerned is no longer competent to make them. (This is now legal in all states, although not in the District of Columbia.) Here again, the appointed person may be a relative, physician or legal or religious adviser, and here too confusion and quarrels may be avoided by conferring the necessary authority in advance.

Economics of Dying

There is, finally, the question of money, which plays a part in even this sort of decision. Many people were shocked last year when Governor Richard D. Lamm of Colorado urged people who had no real prospect of life to "get out of the way" and stop using resources that could be used more profitably by other people. This sounds callous, and it probably was, but it was the truth. We have not yet reached the point, even in this glorious nation, where living or dying has nothing to do with economics. That is what makes the right to die with dignity an issue of morality as well as policy and law.

Whether we are old or young, healthy or ill, we cannot go on shirking the questions of who shall live, who shall die and who shall decide.

"We believe that so-called 'living wills' are
misnamed, unnecessary and dangerous."

Living Wills
Are Unnecessary

Luke Wilson

Many right-to-life groups oppose living wills because they believe
the documents promote euthanasia, are vaguely worded, and are
legally redundant. In the following viewpoint, Luke Wilson, a
writer for the *Right to Life of Michigan News*, argues that living
wills are a thinly-disguised attempt by right-to-die groups to
weaken existing euthanasia laws. He thinks that living wills imply that the elderly have a "duty to die."

As you read, consider the following questions:

1. In Wilson's opinion, what is the real intention of right-to-
   die groups in creating living wills?
2. Why does he feel living wills are unnecessary?
3. According to the author, why do health care bureaucrats
   support the use of living wills?

Luke Wilson, "Allowing To Die, or Aiming To Kill," *Right to Life of Michigan News*,
May/June 1986. Reprinted with the author's permission.

The so-called "Living Will" has become virtually a household word in the last few years. It is presented as a simple legal document by which an individual sets down for his physician advanced directives for the future withdrawal of even such basic care as a feeding tube, should he be stricken with disease or illness and become unable to make medical decisions for himself.

But an increasing number of legal, medical and religious experts are labeling it a "death contract;" a tool spawned directly by the organized euthanasia movement to open the door for legalizing assisted suicide, direct euthanasia, and the dumping of America's dependent elderly.

Michigan has not passed legislation recognizing "Living Wills." However, several measures to provide legal recognition to these dangerous documents have been introduced in the Michigan Legislature. . . .

Deception of Living Wills

Right to Life of Michigan stands totally opposed to this kind of legislation because we believe that so-called "living wills" are misnamed, unnecessary and dangerous. By law, competent patients already have the right to refuse medical treatment—"living wills" do not expand this right; but alarmingly, in the case of patients unable to make medical decisions for themselves, they cut family members completely out of their traditional decision-making role, and can facilitate the deliberate killing through neglect of dependent patients, especially the elderly.

It is impossible to evaluate the so-called "Living Will" in a vacuum—it is vital to consider its origin, and the historical circumstances in which it has gained popularity.

The "Living Will" was the brainchild not of patients' rights advocates or the senior citizens movement, but of the *organized euthanasia movement*.

It was first introduced at a 1967 meeting of the euthanasia education council by one of the group's members, Luis Kutner. As an article in the Euthanasia Education Council's newsletter candidly admits, the "Living Will" was explicitly devised as a softening up strategy to overcome society's rightful abhorrence of legalizing assisted suicide and mercy-killing:

> Because no euthanasia bill had ever been passed, members of the (Euthanasia) Society gave serious thought to *the need to create a climate in which such legislation might be possible . . . the publicity given to the Living . . . helped to promote discussion of euthanasia.* (*Euthanasia News,* November, 1975)

Those who are inclined to quickly dismiss as alarmist the view that "living wills" are a Trojan horse by which the Euthanasia movement is working to legalize mercy killing and assisted suicide should listen to the warning of Prof. Yale Kamisar of the University of Michigan Law School. Kamisar, one of the country's preeminent authorities in constitutional and criminal law, has been tracking the progress of the euthanasia movement for 30 years.

"Well, maybe it [euthanasia] can not [happen here]; but no small part of our Constitution and no small number of our Supreme Court opinions stem from the fear that *it can happen here unless we darn well make sure that it does not* by adamantly holding the line, by swiftly snuffing out what are or might be small beginnings of what we do not want to happen here. To flick off . . . the fears about legalized euthanasia as so much nonsense, as a chimerical 'parade of horrors,' is to sweep away much of the ground on which all our civil liberties rest."

Verbal Engineering

Ethicist Dr. William Smith points out that "social engineering is always preceded by verbal engineering." Words are the ultimate tactics, and nowhere is this better illustrated than in the subtle mask of euphemisms devised by the organized euthanasia movement to separate the idea of killing from its goals of legalizing assisted suicide and euthanasia.

A Vehicle for Euthanasia

"Living wills are not needed. Even euthanasia advocates are quite aware of that fact. Yet they push the same because they view living wills as good vehicles to precondition physicians and patients to the approval of euthanasia (mercy killing)."

Clifford Bajema, *Right to Life of Michigan News*, May-June 1986.

First, The Euthanasia Education Council discreetly, but deceptively changed its name in 1978 to Concern for Dying. Its companion organization, founded in 1938 as the Euthanasia Society of America, underwent a similar public relations facelift in 1975 when it changed its name to the Society for the Right to Die.

While these groups took the term euthanasia out of their names, there is no basis for thinking that their historic goals of legalizing assisted suicide and the deliberate killing of the institutionalized incompetent—carefully documented by Prof. Yale Kamisar of the University of Michigan Law School—have changed. And they have devised their own vocabulary to cleverly promote deliberate killing without ever using the word:

• Suicide becomes "self deliverance"
• Assisted suicide is "deliverance"

• Killing by injection is "aid in dying"
• A document that requires a doctor to kill by neglect a diabetic patient by withholding insulin or a feeding tube is a "living will"
There is a word for this. GOOBLEY-GOOK!

The strategy of the euthanasia advocates is to confuse the public with terminology, hit them over the head with hard cases, and then clamor for legislation like the "living will" that is unwise, unnecessary and dangerous. . . .

The Right Already Exists

Several important facts about patients' rights are often ignored in the present confusion about medical decision-making.

First, patients already have a legally recognized right to refuse medical treatment. This goes back to Common Law tradition, and is unquestioned. When a patient is incapacitated and cannot make medical decisions for himself, the attending physician in consultation with family members makes medical decisions for the patient, including those to withdraw treatment.

Second, neither present law nor the moral position of any church or right to life organization require that every form of treatment be applied to every patient in every circumstance. If a patient is imminently dying, it is both good medicine and good morals to withdraw useless treatment that would only prolong the dying process with no benefit to the patient. Key points here are that:
• The patient will then die of the underlying terminal condition, not starvation or the lack of basic medical care
• Medical treatment is being withdrawn based on a *medical judgement* that death is imminent, and not a *value judgement* that the patient is "better off dead"
• Food and water are still provided as comfort care, except in the closing days for the rare patient for whom this may actually increase discomfort

Killing the Terminally Ill

No change in our laws is necessary to stop useless medical treatment for patients who are not imminently dying. What would require a change, however, and what the "Living Will" facilitates, is a policy of deliberate killing by neglect and starvation of patients suffering from terminal but treatable diseases, or those judged by a doctor to have a "quality of life no longer worth living."

Against the backdrop of economic pressures, the risk of premature and incorrect diagnosis is very real, according to Edward L. Moorhead, M.D. of Grand Rapids, a nationally known cancer treatment specialist, and immediate past president of the National Association of Community Cancer Centers.

Dr. Moorhead told *RLM News* in a recent interview, "A lot of times whether you're 'terminal' depends on who your doctor is.

158

I've seen patients who were told they had three months to live, and 10 years later their doctor is dead and they're still looking good."

The "Living Will" sends a message to our elderly that they have a "duty to die" and get out of the way so younger people can have a better life, as Gov. Richard Lamm of Colorado put it in a 1984 speech.

That some bureaucrats are promoting the "living will" as a means of reducing medical costs is evidenced by a 1979 memo written by a top financial analyst in the Department of Health, Education and Welfare. The memo suggested pressuring states to pass "living will" legislation, claiming that such laws in all 50 states could save the government $1.2 billion a year.

Living Wills Do Not Discriminate

Living will or right-to-die legislation favors death as a solution to difficult, human problems. It ignores the individual circumstances and desires that should determine the nature of terminal care. It promotes attitudes that the elderly and infirm are financial and emotional burdens on society. It removes dying, disability and death from the context of love, life and meaning.

Mary Senander, *Minneapolis Star and Tribune,* March 21, 1985.

University of Chicago professor of medicine, Mark Siegler is among those warning that so-called "death with dignity" legislation is being promoted by some health care bureaucrats to force doctors and nurses to dump the poor and elderly.

Seeds of Abuse

At a medical ethics conference in Minneapolis . . . Dr. Siegler said that doctors and nurses are being pressured to "speed up dying." Siegler noted that the move toward a policy of denying food and water, "plants seeds of great abuse." . . .

There is a real danger that all the hype today about "living wills" is sending a not so subtle message to the sick and elderly. A message that they do have a "duty to die" and let the rest of us get on with living.

Perhaps the question we really ought to be asking ourselves is, For the emotional and moral health of our society, can we afford to tamper with the legal safeguards that insure adequate medical care and protection for the aged and sickly in our midst?

"It is not unethical to discontinue all means of life-prolonging medical treatment."

The Courts Should Allow the Withdrawal of Life Support

Neal R. Peirce and the American Medical Association

In 1975 the US Supreme Court decided that Karen Ann Quinlan's family had a right to end her connection to mechanical life-support systems. That right is now widely accepted for the families of terminally ill patients. Families of terminally ill patients have added a new twist by seeking the right to end all medical treatment for dying loved ones. In Part I of the following viewpoint, Neal R. Peirce, a syndicated columnist, argues that terminally ill patients should be allowed to refuse medical treatment, including forced feeding. Part II is a guideline released by the Council on Judicial and Ethical Affairs of the American Medical Association (AMA) on life-prolonging medical treatment.

As you read, consider the following questions:

1. According to Peirce, who ultimately pays the bill for keeping terminally ill patients alive?
2. What are the "radical" proposals Peirce mentions?

Neal R. Peirce, "Right-To-Life Groups Fail To Recognize the Right To Die," *Minneapolis Star and Tribune*, February 3, 1985. © 1985, Washington Post Writers Group, reprinted with permission.
Reprinted from *Current Opinions of the Council on Ethical and Judicial Affairs of the American Medical Association*, 1986, with permission of the American Medical Association.

"A slippery slope" . . . "starving patients to death" . . . "a legalized death wish" . . . "doses of death" . . . "playing God by ending life prematurely."

Those are just some of the epithets that the "right-to-life" movement is throwing, not at its familiar target of abortion, but at the tough new "choice" issue facing state legislatures: whether terminally ill people or their families have the right to say "no" to artificial life support.

Wrenching as it is, the decision about an abortion confronts only a small minority of American families. But millions—perhaps most of us—will one day be asked to stave off death, for ourselves or for loved ones, by use of the medical machines that cleanse blood, breathe for diseased lungs or jolt halted hearts back into action. The "right-to-lifers" may be making a fatal error by challenging all Americans' right to die in peace.

An Enduring Issue

The "right-to-die" issue has been on legislative agendas for almost a decade. Twenty-two states have approved some form of the "living will," which permits competent adults to reject in advance heroic measures to extend their lives artificially. A feature pioneered by Delaware law allows a person signing a living will to designate a proxy—often a family member—to make those difficult decisions if the patient is too ill to make them.

The New Jersey Supreme Court, in a landmark decision, . . . ruled that life-sustaining treatment may be withdrawn from incurable nursing-home patients who are no longer competent to make decisions for themselves. While not binding on other states, the New Jersey court's decision—like its celebrated opinion of a decade ago, permitting withdrawal of respirator treatment in the Karen Ann Quinlan case—may well be a benchmark for courts across the country.

The decision is cautious: When there's no living will or other evidence of what a patient would want done, "It is best to err, if at all, in favor of preserving life." The state ombudsman has to be consulted; two independent physicians and a legal guardian must approve.

Stopping Painful Procedures

But when the conditions are met, invasive painful procedures— even nasal-gastric tubes for forced feeding—can be ended, and the patient may be allowed to die. Many ethicists, clergy and doctors have hailed the decision as a breakthrough for patients' rights.

But personal choice, early or late in life, seems anathema to the "pro-life" lobby. The court decision, said New Jersey Right to Life Committee leader Adolf Schimpf, "conditions society to eliminating all who become inconvenient—the elderly, the handicapped and the retarded." It all amounts, according to the National Right to Life Committee's Dr. Jack Willke, to "a license to empty our nursing homes" by mercy killings of their occupants.

Starvation May Be More Humane

Patients who are allowed to die without artificial hydration and nutrition may well die more comfortably than patients who receive conventional amounts of intravenous hydration. . . .

Thus, those patients whose "need" for artificial nutrition and hydration arises only near the time of death may be harmed by it provision. It is not at all clear that they receive any benefit in having a slightly prolonged life, and it does seem reasonable to allow a surrogate to decide that, for this patient at this time, slight prolongation of life is not warranted if it involves measures that will probably increase the patient's suffering as he or she dies.

Joanne Lynn and James F. Childress, *The Hastings Center Report,* October 1983.

A chief problem the pro-lifers face is the high price—fiscal and social—of preserving all life at all costs. No less than 28 percent of the country's $75 billion yearly Medicare budget is used to maintain the elderly in their last year of life—most of it during the last month. That figure almost equals all federal aid for the nation's jobless. And the crisis is just beginning: Today, 11 percent of Americans are over 65; in 2010, 20 percent of us will be. Prolonging the death of terminal patients easily costs $20,000 to $50,000 a case—bills we all pay through Medicare, Medicaid and private insurance. "Something must be done," Dr. George Crile Jr. of the Cleveland Clinic wrote recently in *USA Today.* "No insurance company, national or private, should be obliged to sustain the hopeless lives of those who wish to die and whose families agree.

Among the more "radical" proposals is that living wills be recognized nationally—not only in the state where they're written—and that they be required for people receiving Medicare benefits. Crile even recommended that families insisting on extraordinary life-sustaining treatment for terminal patients should be required to shoulder the cost themselves. Critics may say that dooms the poor while saving the rich. But it may be the lucky patient who's allowed to die naturally.

Last year a 70-year-old Californian, William Bartling, suffering from five incurable diseases, lingered more than seven months in a Glendale hospital when authorities refused his repeated request to free him from life-support equipment. The combined medical and legal costs, as Bartling fought to die, topped $500,000.

In some states, the right-to-life lobby has killed living-will proposals. Says Walter Kunicki, the 26-year-old state representative and registered nurse who pushed living-will legislation through the Wisconsin Legislature last year: "Certain people said, 'You may not want this out on the floor because the pro-lifers are going to come at you.' I happen to be a Catholic. I'm fortunate to have a very understanding pastor who supports me."

The pro-lifers may find themselves facing a lot more legislators like Kunicki as the idea spreads that adults are entitled to make their own choices. The "radical," new idea is that they have as much a moral and legal right to choose a natural death as they have in deciding whether to go to a doctor in the first place.

II

The social commitment of the physician is to sustain life and relieve suffering. Where the performance of one duty conflicts with the other, the choice of the patient, or his family or legal representative if the patient is incompetent to act in his own behalf, should prevail. In the absense of the patient's choice or an authorized proxy, the physician must act in the best interest of the patient.

For humane reasons, with informed consent, a physician may do what is medically necessary to alleviate severe pain, or cease or omit treatment to permit a terminally ill patient whose death is imminent to die. However, he should not intentionally cause death. In deciding whether the administration of potentially life-prolonging medical treatment is in the best interest of the patient who is incompetent to act in his own behalf, the physician should determine what the possibility is for extending life under humane and comfortable conditions and what are the prior expressed wishes of the patient and attitudes of the family or those who have responsibility for the custody of the patient.

Even if death is not imminent but a patient's coma is beyond doubt irreversible and there are adequate safeguards to confirm the accuracy of the diagnosis and with the concurrence of those who have responsibility for the care of the patient, it is not unethical to discontinue all means of life-prolonging medical treatment.

Life-prolonging medical treatment includes medication and artificially or technologically supplied respiration, nutrition or hydration. In treating a terminally ill or irreversibly comatose patient, the physician should determine whether the benefits of treatment outweigh its burdens. At all times, the dignity of the patient should be maintained.

"The courts are creating a formula for death that is unbelievably potent."

The Courts Should Not Allow the Withdrawal of Life Support

David H. Andrusko

Right-to-life groups often fight their battles in American courts. Two famous examples are the *Roe v. Wade* abortion case and the Karen Ann Quinlan euthanasia case. Many right-to-life groups believe these court decisions were a setback in fighting for the sanctity of life. David H. Andrusko is editor of *National Right to Life News,* a pro-life publication. He argues that US courts are encouraging active euthanasia by ruling in favor of cutting off life support, including nutrition, to terminally ill patients.

As you read, consider the following questions:

1. Why does the author believe a "Pandora's box" has been opened by the New Jersey Supreme Court's decision?
2. What role does Andrusko say the American Medical Association statement plays in courts' decisions?
3. Why does the author argue that the courts are making more groups "vulnerable"?

David H. Andrusko, "Who Is Next?" *National Right to Life News,* May 15, 1986. Reprinted with permission.

No pro-lifer who soberly contemplates the recent spate of court cases authorizing the withdrawal of food and water from helpless patients can help but feel almost overwhelmed. Lord, how quickly awful things are coming to pass. It seems as if the real sentiments of judges were buried in the early cases but that their gut-level feelings now are coming to the surface. For example, in the cases handed down in early 1985, judges at least bothered to mumble words of reassurance: they conceded how difficult condemning patients to a ghastly death by starvation and dehydration was on our consciences . . . but concluded, nevertheless . . . such is death. Of late, while many judges still retain this pose of reluctance, it is abundantly clear that a significant minority are growing impatient. Their tolerance for those having trouble stomaching such inhumane behavior is waning. . . .

Consider: it has been barely two and one-half years since the campaign to find justifications to deny food and water floated its first trial balloons. Predictably, the first soundings from a creditable source were taken by the euthanasia movement's intellectual troubleshooter, the Hastings Center. It took the form of an October 1983 article written by Joanne Lynn and James Childress, titled "Must Patients Always Be Given Food and Water?" Needless to say, the answer was a resounding "No!" . . .

The Slide to Auschwitz

Almost all of the recent setbacks came our way courtesy of the courts. The transitional legal case in what Surgeon General C. Everett Koop once prophetically called the Slide to Auschwitz probably was the Claire Conroy case handed down by the New Jersey Supreme Court Jan. 17, 1985. I say transitional because on three different levels the *Conroy* decision *seemed* to be tightly drawn. First, in the absence of clear evidence that the now-incompetent patient had previously indicated he would not desire nutrition and hydration, under *Conroy* the patient would have to be in a dreadful state before food and water could be withdrawn. Second, the New Jersey Supreme Court specifically excluded "quality of life" considerations when computing the "benefits" and "burdens" to the patient of continuing to live. And third, the court held that its decisions applied only to the facts and circumstances presented in the *Conroy* case—an elderly nursing home patient suffering from serious and permanent mental and physical impairments and who would probably die within a year even with treatment and care.

Yet I remember vividly my first reaction to reading news accounts of the *Conroy* verdict. I am by nature the very opposite

165

THE SUPREME COURT AND THE TIDE

John J. Knudsen. Reprinted with permission.

of a fatalist but I knew in my bones that a Pandora's box had been thrown wide open. Once we find a category of impaired people "eligible" for non-treatment, there is simply no place to logically stop. If (as was held in the *Conroy* case) to "qualify" for nontreatment, no one must be permanently mentally impaired, be in a nursing home, be elderly, and be likely to die within a year, who is to say that if a patient fulfills only three of the criteria he oughtn't to be killed? Indeed, what's to say you need be brain-damaged? For that matter, as is the case with Elizabeth Bouvia, why do you have to be dying to "exercise your constitutional right to forego the use of artificial life sustaining measures"?

"Life-Sustaining Treatment"

It is instructive that the Lynn/Childress essay was rife with the kind of pseudo-tough mindedness that is becoming the language of choice for appellate judges and so-called "ethicists." Sure, they concede, it's a bit hard on the nerves to watch patients withering away before your very eyes but that misses the point. And what *is* the point? Well, that aesthetics aside, there is no "morally relevant" way in which food and water are distinguishable from any other "life-sustaining medical treatment." Those of us who think otherwise are locked into a mode of moral reasoning rendered obsolete by modern high-tech medicine. Apologists for this inhumanity (and they are legion) agree it may indeed be hard on the rest of us (the horrible fate of the poor patient is conveniently overlooked), but such is the price we pay for facing up to "difficult choices."

The principle obstacle to an unimpeded slide down the slippery slope to active euthanasia was the absence of an unambiguous go-ahead sign from the American Medical Association. However, once the AMA decided . . . that it is ethical for doctors to withhold even food and water from irreversibly comatose patients, those justices panting to withdraw treatment anyway glommed onto the AMA's imprimatur as unequivocal support for their decisions. Look, they said, we are doing nothing that the leading medical organization in this country wouldn't approve of. And, of course, it is the nature of such gigantic societal changes that matters do not just come to a screeching stop. They continue to evolve. For instance, as surely as night follows day, in the next year, a number of new recommendations and/or judicial decisions will come down extending and solidifying the new ethic. To name just a few: first, in the *very* near future, there will be a hue and cry that it is cruel/unjust/unconstitutional/ageist to make the patients suffer. Better they be given a lethal injection. Second, offing patients is a bit avant garde to be done publicly. Why not convert unused maternity wings into designated . . . expiration centers? And, of course, why let perfectly good organs go to waste? We must have legislation authorizing the harvesting of hearts and livers and kidneys from patients about to have their "right to privacy" exercised for them. Fourth (under the Bouvia case reasoning), if a competent patient has a constitutional right to commit suicide by starving themselves to death with the aid of hospital personnel, it would be unconstitutional to deny the same right to incompetent patients. Therefore, those people with, let us say, Alzheimer's disease must be assisted to exercise their right to refuse treatment. And fifth (again employing the reasoning on display in the Bouvia case), if the "meaninglessness" of the patient's life adds still more weight to their right to kill themselves—er, exercised their right to forego treatment—then is it not simple fairness to encourage in the strongest possible terms other patients living similarly meaningless lives to come to grips with the pointlessness of their existence and exit gracefully?

Facing the Pro-Death Juggernaut

Hyperbole? Fear-mongering? I just wish it were so. Indeed, matters may be even worse than I suggest. The courts are creating a formula for death that is unbelievably potent. On the one hand, courts are using the federal and state constitutions to "constitutionalize" the right to withdraw treatment. (As you would expect, this "right" derives directly from the "right to privacy.") On the other hand, they are recognizing a growing number of legal mechanisms to extend this right to incompetent patients—living wills, substituted judgment, power of attorney, etc. This legal elixir means that more and more vulnerable groups are in mortal danger from a court system intoxicated with the power of exercising for patients a "right" discovered lurking in the penumbras of various amendments to the Constitution less than 20 years ago. As we hunker down for this the most difficult battle the Movement will likely ever face, let us not kid ourselves. We face a pro-death juggernaut that will require every ounce of our creativity, resolve, and determination to repulse.

The Ability To Empathize

The ability to empathize, to see a situation from another person's vantage point, is an important skill. When we empathize, we put ourselves in someone else's position. This helps us to look at a problem in a way that we perhaps have not considered before. The ability to understand an opponent's viewpoint is a difficult skill, one that is needed for a highly emotional and controversial subject like euthanasia.

Should people be allowed to choose the method of their death if death is indeed imminent? Should others be allowed to aid in death, or should they let nature take its course? These ethical questions will never receive answers that satisfy everyone. Religious background, personal philosophy, and life experiences all become factors in making such decisions.

In this activity you will be asked to decide what makes a life worth living and whether or not to end the lives of people who are close to death. Three case studies will be presented in which you must decide what should be done with people who have little hope of regaining control of their once-healthy bodies.

Part I

The first part of this activity will be done individually. After studying the values listed below, rank them according to what you think is most important in deciding whether or not to pull the plug on life-support systems. Use number 1 for the most important factor, number 2 for the second most important factor, and so on.

_____ the patient's quality of life
_____ emotional anguish of the family
_____ the patient's previously spoken desire not to live in a comatose state
_____ financial costs of keeping the patient alive
_____ putting an end to the patient's suffering

Part II

Keep in mind the values you deemed most important in deciding whether to continue or withdraw life support. The class should then break into groups of three or four students. Study each of the following cases carefully and discuss within your group what you would do. Come to a consensus before moving on to the next example. When your group has discussed all three cases, present your answers to the class and be ready to defend your decisions. There will be no completely correct or incorrect answers, only opinions on the priorities you think are most important.

_____1. Harriet is an 80-year-old woman who needs open-heart surgery but refuses because she says she's "too old." A person of vitality, Harriet has lost her energy and zest for life as her weak heart gets progressively worse. She refuses food orally, so life-sustaining tubes are forced down her throat, through her nose, and into her veins against her will. She implores you, as her daughter, to let her die a peaceful death. What do you do?

_____2. Mike is a healthy 25-year-old man who enjoys hobbies such as motorcycle riding, windsurfing, and camping. Mike gets in a motorcycle accident that leaves him paralyzed and in a coma from which the doctors say he may or may not recover. Mike doesn't need a respirator, but he does need to be fed intravenously. You are Mike's father. Should you ask that food and hydration be stopped to bring about death, or do you wait, hoping that Mike comes out of the coma?

_____3. Marvin has suffered a stroke that has left him comatose. The doctors say the 70-year-old man has no recordable brain activity and his brain stem is severely damaged. Since Marvin had no health coverage, sustaining Marvin's life is a financial burden on his wife, Doris. She loves Marvin but believes that the man she married is now gone; only his body remains. Should Doris disconnect Marvin's life-support system to save herself tens of thousands of dollars?

Periodical Bibliography

The following list of periodical articles deals with the subject matter of this chapter.

Harold O.J. Brown — "Euthanasia: Drawing New Distinctions," *Journal of Christian Nursing*, Fall 1986.

Evan R. Collins Jr. — "The Right to Choose Life or Death," *USA Today*, November 1984.

The Economist — "Nunc Dimittis," May 17, 1986.

Alvan R. Feinstein — "Why Won't the Doctors Let Her Die?" *The New York Times*, October 6, 1986.

Evan Gahr — "'Living Wills' Pull Plug on Needless Suffering," *National Catholic Reporter*, April 29, 1986.

Ellen Goodman — "Letting Death Come Isn't the Same Thing as Killing," *Los Angeles Times*, March 28, 1986.

Nat Hentoff — "Barriers Against Killing Are Coming Down," *National Right to Life News*, April 10, 1986.

Jane D. Hoyt — "A 'New Ethic' for the 'New Medicine'?" *Human Life Issues*, Spring 1986.

Francis I. Kane — "Keeping Elizabeth Bouvia Alive for the Public Good," *Hastings Center Report*, December 1985.

John J. Paris — "When Burdens of Feeding Outweigh Benefits," *Hastings Center Report*, February 1986.

Philip R. Reilly — "Physician Defends Feeding Man in Coma," *American Medical News*, February 14, 1986.

Barbara Reynolds — "Doctors Shouldn't Kill Patients They Can't Cure," (interview with Anne E. Bannon), *USA Today*, April 2, 1986.

Roger Rosenblatt — "The Quality of Mercy Killing," *Time*, August 26, 1985.

Joseph R. Stanton — "The New Untermenschen," *The Human Life Review*, Fall 1985.

Cal Thomas — "Is Euthanasia the Next Step in a Better Quality of Life?" *Los Angeles Times*, October 8, 1984.

Do the Dying Need Alternative Care?

death
and dying

> *"Hospitals are committed to curing sick people, and this does not necessarily include helping people to die well. The hospital staff . . . often do not know how to cope with the 'failures'— the hopelessly ill."*

Hospitals Cannot Cope with Dying Patients

John S. Stephenson

During the 1970s, the way hospitals respond to dying patients became a major issue. Many people argued that hospitals ignore the needs of terminally ill patients: hospitals' technology and staff are geared toward curing people, rather than toward helping them die well. As an alternative, a hospice movement formed in the United States and began working to establish a system of care with the goal of making dying patients as comfortable as possible. John S. Stephenson argues in the following viewpoint that hospitals are bureaucratic organizations set up to cure sick people and make money. He concludes that they cannot help the dying as well as hospices can.

As you read, consider the following questions:

1. According to the author, what are the goals and purposes of modern hospitals?
2. How does he believe those goals affect the dying patient?
3. What is the author's opinion of hospices within hospitals?

The goal of a hospital is to provide health care for members of the community. In order to do this in the most efficient way possible, the contemporary hospital is bureaucratically organized. This form of organization has ramifications for patient care and management. This rational system can be highly beneficial, as experts can bring the latest medical knowledge to bear in the fight against disease, but oftentimes the *person* becomes lost in the maze of technology and bureaucracy. Hospital patients report feelings of loneliness and being less than human, and can become angered at being referred to as "the peptic ulcer" or "the broken leg." The hospital staff, immersed in the world of medicine, combating disease, and helping in the healing process, may lose sight of the individual person and see only the symptoms. . . .

Coping with the "Failures"

Of further importance for our particular interests is the fact that hospitals are committed to curing sick people, and this does not necessarily include helping people to die well. The hospital staff has been trained to cure; to defeat death. They often do not know how to cope with the "failures"—the hopelessly ill and dying.

The following description of an eighty-year-old terminally ill woman's experience in a hospital is typical of many such accounts:

> She was isolated behind drawn curtains, and when the interviewer intruded, she pleaded, "Please come talk to me." During her 35-day stay in the hospital she was cared for by 38 different nurses. Except for three days in July, Miss R was never cared for by the same nurse on two consecutive days. Of the 105 nursing shifts during her hospital stay, the nurses recorded her status only for 66 shifts, and only nine of the nurse's notes mentioned her psychological pain, that she was very lonely, crying all day, depressed, asking to die, afraid of everything. Because she was continually calling for a nurse to rectify her isolation, nurses responded to her call bell with increasing delay, avoiding her as much as possible. The resident physicians on ward rounds were found to spend only an average of one minute in Miss R's room, none got close enough to touch her, and only rarely did anyone speak to her. She begged the student observer to stay with her, after he held her hand and listened to her talk. She pleaded: "Help me, you are not like the others, help me." The staff laughed nervously in discussing the fact that she once called the police for help. She voiced suicidal thoughts of trying to jump out the window, and the staff reaction was an expressed wish to get her moved out of the ward to a nursing home, because they found her care so troublesome. . . .

It is important within the context of our investigation . . . [of the

174

hospital] to keep in mind that we are examining the behavior of individuals caught up in the values and priorities of a larger social system. It is not my contention that individuals working in large bureaucratic organizations are less responsive to the human needs of their patients. What is important is that we become aware of the subtle ways in which the demands of the bureaucracy force bureaucratic personnel to act in ways which are perhaps counter to the human needs of the dying patient. For example, efforts by nurses and doctors to eliminate family members from the death-bed scene may not be strictly in response to their own selfish desires, but may be influenced by the fact that the ward is so heavily understaffed that to respond fully to the needs of the dying patient would severely limit the functioning of the hospital staff in other areas of their work responsibilities. A hospital is basically an economic institution. If it does not operate efficiently or at a profit it could be shut down. Therefore, in the context of a hospital, efficiency, profit, and money motive can tend to become more important than human needs of the patient. . . . Wolf Heyderbrand, in his book *Hospital Bureaucracy*, stated that the hospital "must provide the setting or framework in which the principles and practices of modern business and technology can be successfully related to the standards and imagery of 'helping peo-

"The artificial life support systems are intact, but I'd say Mr. Phipps could use a talking to."

ple' as derived from ethical precepts, social and psychological insights, and medical practice.''

Heyderbrand's statement is an idealistic one, for the values of business and those of helping people may often be in conflict. When those values of business and technology supersede the more humanistic ones, the patient may suffer as a result. The human needs of the patient become subordinate to the bureaucratic demands of the hospital system, leaving the patient feeling depersonalized and alienated from the very system which, ironically, was designed to help him. . . .

Cure More Important than Care

The combination of the bureaucratic needs of the hospital organization and the biomedical model which sees death as pathological and not natural, often supersedes the care needs of the patient. The ''cure goal'' has become institutionalized in the hospital, and is more important than the ''goal of care.'' This is not to imply that hospital physicians and staff are uncaring, but rather that the organization in which they work is not oriented primarily toward patient care as much as it is to saving lives and controlling death. The result has been the depersonalization and objectification of the patient in the cause of bureaucratic efficiency and improved medical technology. . . .

The Hospice as an Alternative

The concept of the hospice originally developed in Ireland, where the Sisters of Charity organized homes for the dying poor. Today, the ideal hospice has three components: 1) a staff devoted to home care for those patients who are able to stay in their homes, 2) outpatient services, and 3) an inpatient facility. Those forming teams to care for the dying in their homes are available twenty-four hours a day, so that the patients do not feel that they are alone or without others who care about them. The teams are just that, and lack a rigid, hierarchical authority structure. . . .

The goals of the hospice are the management of pain symptoms and meeting the social, psychological, and spiritual needs of the dying person. Also, many hospices treat the aged and infirm. . . .

In the hospice, medical systems and caretaking functions give way to concern for the total needs of the dying person and those around him. While recognizing professional competencies, the hospice replaces the impersonal goals of medical science (hospitals) and profit making (nursing homes) with a humanistic concern for the quality of life of the dying.

A caveat is necessary here: For the most part, the hospice movement is still in its formative stage. Few organizations have reached a point of achieving all three of the goals mentioned earlier. . . .

Whether the hospice concept can survive in its pure form is a matter of conjecture. Already the demands of funding agencies have forced changes in the organizational structures of some hospices which may be seen as pushing the organizations toward a closer approximation of bureaucracy.

Hospice and Protest

In looking at the history of the hospice movement in the United States, one finds indications that the movement arose in protest to the treatment of the dying in hospitals and nursing homes. Experiencing such treatment, professionals who sought better care for the dying found the hospice model offered a better solution than hospitals and nursing homes. However, as is so often the case in American society, feasibility is measured in dollars and cents. For many in the hospice movement, the success of the hospice seems to be measured in terms of the ability of the particular group to raise funds. Because 95 percent of Americans are insured by some form of medical insurance, the fledgling hospice organizations have had to contend with a lack of recognition by health insurance companies. Insurance companies do not, as a rule, pay for "bereavement care or many of the social work functions" that are carried out by hospices. Other factors, such as rival service providers, licensing boards, and special interest groups, have put pressure upon the hospice movement to legitimize itself in terms of bureaucratic standards and the medical model. As a result, it may be that the hospice model will not survive in its present form.

Prolonging Life at Any Cost

In America, . . . physicians and nurses are committed to prolonging life at almost any cost. They are trained to use everything at their command, from sophisticated technology to advanced medication therapy, to keep the patient alive—no matter what the quality of that life is. To many practitioners, impending death represents failure. Because health care personnel usually experience so much anxiety in caring for the dying patient, they often take refuge in doing the routine, technical, and impersonal tasks involved in patient care, in order to keep from developing a personal relationship with that patient. Often physicians and nurses avoid the dying patient if at all possible.

Elizabeth Gilman McNulty and Robert A. Holderly, *Hospice, A Caring Challenge*, 1983.

One alternative form being implemented in several places is the formation of a hospice within a hospital. Objections to this include differences in philosophies, placing the dying in the same environment as those recovering from illness, the different training required by the two organizations, and the negative views of the hospice concept held by many hospital staff members. Arguments in favor state that there are many hospitals with extra space available, the hospital's vast resources could be available for the hospice staff, and that the hospice approach can bring about changes in the attitudes of the entire hospital staff.

From a sociological perspective, it seems naive to expect that an organization so radically different from the larger parent organization is going to survive intact. Attempts at innovation within organizations, when those innovations imply changes in roles or values, often meet with both resistance and efforts to bring about conformity to the goals and values of the parent organization. Without financial independence, it is doubtful that the hospice concept will be able to survive intact.

Opposing Dominant Values

The hospice idea is often characterized by those involved as a "movement." This term implies a certain amount of idealism and ideology, as well as an orientation toward action. The implementation of the hospice ideology, whose humanistic values run counter to many of the dominant American values, will face many challenges both directly (opposition from interest groups such as professional organizations and governmental bureaucracies) and indirectly (competition within the larger hospital organizations). The success or failure of the movement will depend not only on the leadership ability of those involved in the hospice movement but also on the ability of the larger society to accept or at least tolerate an organization whose humanistic and death-accepting values are so opposed to the dominant values in American life.

"*By constantly seeking to minimize the endemic 'depersonalization' of the [hospital] institution, hospice staff can serve as a model for the institution.*"

Hospitals Can Effectively Respond to the Dying

Ina Ajemian and Balfour Mount

After being criticized for being insensitive to dying patients, some hospitals developed special units, modeled after the hospice concept, to care for the dying. The authors of the following viewpoint, Ina Ajemian and Balfour Mount, developed one of the first hospice units within a hospital. In the viewpoint, they describe a terminal care unit at Royal Victoria Hospital in Canada. By combining hospice and hospital, patients get both excellent palliative care (care designed to alleviate pain) and the comprehensive service and technology hospitals have to offer. The authors teach at McGill University School of Medicine in Montreal, Canada.

As you read, consider the following questions:

1. What are some of the goals the authors describe of hospice/palliative care units in hospitals?
2. How do hospice units benefit hospitals, according to Ajemian and Mount?
3. How do they say hospice units in hospitals benefit dying patients?

From *The Hospice: Development and Administration,* Second edition, edited by Glen W. Davidson, © 1985. With permission from Hemisphere Publishing Corporation, New York, Washington DC.

During the last decade, two facts have become evident: the care of the terminally ill has been grossly deficient in our modern health care system, and their needs can be met more effectively with special services designed to complement services in the traditional health care system. With 70 percent of today's patients dying in institutions, the extent of these problems cannot be minimized.

The hundreds of hospice/palliative care programs established in the last ten years in response to this challenge have a number of factors which depart from the traditional mode.

• Whole person care is mandatory. Excellence in pain and symptom control is the foundation for emphasis on psychological, social, and spiritual issues.

• Both patients and their families are considered in setting goals of care.

• Bereavement support for key family members is considered to be an integral part of comprehensive terminal care programs.

• Every effort is made in an inpatient setting to minimize "institutional depersonalization" and to foster individuality, informality and a home-like lifestyle.

• Although the uncertainty of prognosis is recognized, terminal care is "life oriented," focusing on the control of symptoms which permits enhanced relationships, reconciliation, sense of fulfillment and personal growth.

• New models of interdisciplinary teams are required to meet such a broad problem mandate, necessitating the development of new patterns of interaction and the inclusion of effective support mechanisms.

The Need for Specialized Care

The Palliative Care Service of the Royal Victoria Hospital represents one attempt to adapt these principles to the needs of a thousand-bed teaching hospital community. The service was instituted in 1975, following a study which underlined the great deficiencies in care of dying patients throughout the hospital. Presently, the service consists of an eighteen-bed inpatient unit, hospital-based home care, a consultation/symptom control team which visits patients throughout the hospital, an outpatient clinic and bereavement follow-up care. . . .

In a time of major economic constraint, it is important to ask whether the development of yet another specialized service for patient care is warranted. Is it not possible to train all hospital and home care staff to give improved terminal care? While recent educational programs in death and dying have increased staff awareness of the particular needs of terminally ill patients and their families, there remains a basic problem: the discrepancy between the orientation of hospitals and the needs of these patients. The training and skills of professional staff in general hospitals are focused toward four ends: investigation, diagnosis, cure and prolongation of life. These activities are largely irrelevant to terminally ill patients—for whom quality of life is the only appropriate goal. . . .

A Hospice Unit in a General Hospital

When, as often happens, the transition from active anti-cancer therapy to palliative care is unclear, difficult or delayed, the presence of the palliative care team within the institution facilitates early involvement, and lessens the trauma attached to the shift in therapeutic goals. In a hospice unit attached to a hospital, resources, such as skilled personnel and specialized equipment (for example, consultant neurologists and radiation therapists), are readily available when needed for symptom alleviation.

Changes in Traditional Care

The non-hospice programmes of care, the traditional doctor in hospital and nursing home programmes of care which many of us despaired of for so long, . . . are now beginning to undergo change and metamorphosis on the basis of what they have seen and learned in hospice systems. On all sides in southern California I see the traditional programmes of care for dying patients in traditional hospitals with traditional doctors, now being expanded and having particular services added to them that were simply not there before—a nurse, a social worker, a counsellor, home care services, transportation or even day hospitals. . . .

That may perhaps be the most significant achievement of all: that the development of hospice programmes has brought about quietly and gradually, but significantly, an improvement and upgrading of the programmes of the care for the dying in the standard, traditional or conventional settings where, in fact, most people die.

Paul Torrens, in *Hospice: The Living Idea*, 1981.

The physical proximity of hospice and acute care units may stimulate improved care in both areas. All too often, as documented by Raymond Duff and August Hollingshead, hospitalization involves a series of dehumanizing events serving to incorporate patients into the procedures of the institution and eventually eliminating all sense of autonomy, identity and status as individuals. The hospice focus on whole person medicine serves as a reminder to the institution at large that patients are unique individuals whose suffering may involve many aspects of their personhood. By constantly seeking to minimize the endemic "depersonalization" of the institution, hospice staff can serve as a model for the institution. Questions of appropriate therapy, when the potential for cure or prolongation of life is slight, are often difficult. Hospice staff, as advocates for patients in their total contexts—physical, social and emotional—can insure that decisions reflect anticipated benefits, weighed against anticipated morbidity in all these spheres. Furthermore, the close liaison between acute care wards and a hospice insures medical peer review of the hospice and provides an inherent accountability. The concern with insuring a high standard of medical competence in the hospice team is thus less problematic in this setting than in a hospice physically separated, and without close affiliation, to a medical center.

Patients and their families may experience an enhanced sense of security and trust if continuing concern is demonstrated in the primary treating institution through the provision of a range of services spanning the whole period from inital diagnosis to bereavement follow-up.

One other advantage of a hospice within a hospital environment is cost. In many parts of North America there is currently under-utilization of hospital beds. The location of hospices in general hospitals avoids many of the costs related to the development of a new facility. In addition, such a unit can maximize the efficiency of utilizing existing inpatient beds. . . .

Hospice Consultation Team in a General Hospital

This type of hospice unit provides service for palliative care patients who are inappropriate for transfer or do not wish to be transferred to hospice units. It may be useful to patients facing death in a variety of hospital settings (for example, oncology or intensive care units, or emergency departments).

Hospice consultation teams may be easier to introduce than hospice units in hospital settings in which space and resources are limited. These teams, working alongside staff throughout the hospitals, can do a great deal to change attitudes toward the terminally ill and their families and improve the skill of staff generally. Team members frequently serve as advocates for patients with hospital staff and administrations. . . .

The goals of the Palliative Care Service are the relief of suffering and the enhancement of life. . . .

Certain principles will guide hospice staff in their attempts to diminish the suffering of patients.

Diagnostic and therapeutic goals must be set in terms of the patients and not their diseases. For example, prolonged courses of radiotherapy which change the ultimate prognosis very little cannot be justified since they may simply be increasing discomfort, fears, length of hospital stays, and costs. On the other hand, prompt radiotherapy in spinal cord compression, for example, may avert paraplegia, thus preventing a blow to independent functioning. Blood transfusion rarely improves the quality of life for bedbound patients, but may enable an ambulatory patient to function more fully. To choose which therapy is appropriate requires considerable knowledge of the particular patient, the particular disease, and the particular situation.

All efforts should be made to maximize patients' functions and not their length of life. This frequently implies reducing hospital stays to a minimum, and teaching families to provide care. It may require taking some risks, such as allowing ambulation where the possibility of pathological fracture exists or using nonsteroidal anti-inflammatory drugs and steroids for pain relief and to provide enhanced patient well-being even if there is a risk of perforating ulcer.

Every effort should be made to actively minimize suffering. This requires that competent physicians exercise skill in correctly diagnosing the physiological mechanism underlying patients' physical symptoms, and in manipulating the various drug and other treatment modalities to achieve relief. There is no place in the hospice concept for substandard medical care.

As every aspect of personhood—physical, emotional, social and spiritual—may suffer loss and injury, hospice staff must be prepared to intervene in any aspect. Their relationships with patients and their knowledge of the personhood of each provides the vehicle for diagnosing suffering and intervening effectively. . . .

Patients as Team Members

Patients and key persons (families and others at significant risk in bereavement) are integral members of the health care team on the PCU. This fact is symbolic of the differences in direction between palliative and acute care wards. The significance of their inclusion on the team lies not only in the need to consult and obtain active input from them in drawing up the plan of care, but also in the need to include them as "caregivers" (and not just receivers) to the extent they wish. Such a policy serves to counter the institutional depersonalization many of these patients have experienced. It also assists the key persons in their anticipatory grief.

"No significant differences were noted between the [hospice and hospital] patient groups in measures of pain, symptoms, [or] activities of daily living."

Hospitals and Hospices Are Equally Effective in Treating the Dying

Robert L. Kane, Jeffrey Wales, Leslie Bernstein, Arleen Leibowitz, and Stevan Kaplan

The following viewpoint is an excerpt from a well-known report about medical treatment in hospices and hospitals. Robert L. Kane and several associates at the UCLA School of Medicine compared patients receiving hospice care at a Veterans Administration hospital with patients receiving conventional care. They found no significant differences in the quality of the care and conclude that hospices may have encouraged and educated hospital staff to sensitively treat the dying.

As you read, consider the following questions:

1. What claims do hospice supporters make in favor of hospices, according to the authors?
2. Why do the authors believe hospice care should be a matter of choice?
3. How may hospice care have affected conventional care, according to the authors?

Robert L. Kane, Jeffrey Wales, Leslie Bernstein, Arleen Leibowitz, and Stevan Kaplan "A Randomized Controlled Trial of Hospice Care," *The Lancet*, April 21, 1984. Reprinted with permission.

Terminally ill cancer patients at a Veterans Administration hospital were randomly assigned to receive hospice or conventional care. The hospice care was provided both in a special inpatient unit and at home. 137 hospice patients and 110 control patients and their familial care givers (FCGs) were followed until the patient's death. No significant differences were noted between the patient groups in measures of pain, symptoms, activities of daily living, or affect. Hospice patients expressed more satisfaction with the care they received; and hospice patients' FCGs showed somewhat more satisfaction and less anxiety than did those of controls. Hospice care was not associated with a reduced use of hospital inpatient days or therapeutic procedures and was at least as expensive as conventional care.

Profound Change

Medicine has undergone a profound change in the way it cares for the dying. Spurred by the work of thanatologists, medical personnel have become more concerned about the quality of patients' last days of life. This transition has resulted in the evolution of the hospice. Pioneered in the United Kingdom in the late 1960s, this institution represents a commitment to palliative and supportive care for those patients whose terminal status can be forecast, usually cancer patients. In the United States there has been intense interest in the hospice. A General Accounting Office study in 1979 identified 59 organisations providing hospice-type care, with 73 more in the planning stages. A survey by the Joint Commission on Accreditation of Hospitals indicated that in early 1983 there were 1100-1200 hospice programmes in the United States. These programmes may be either hospital-based or free-standing and may use home care, institutional care, or some combination of the two.

The enthusiasm for hospice care, stimulated by the growing recognition of the importance of care for the dying and a parallel concern about the costs of terminal care, is based primarily on anecdotal data. Claims have been made for benefits including better pain control, fewer symptoms, improved affect, and greater satisfaction with care. The early attempts to evaluate hospice care were limited essentially to descriptive studies. A large national quasi-experimental study of hospice care is underway to address the differences in outcomes achieved by different modes of hospice care associated with the various ways of funding such care. Such investigations must contend with questions about self-selection of hospice patients and the difficulties of identifying comparable controls. Here we present data collected in a randomised

TABLE I-Utilisation of Services

Service	Mean no per subject*	
	Hospice	Control
Total inpatient days	51.0	47.5
General medical	13.2	20.7
Hospice	29.2	—
Intensive care unit	0.2	0.3
Intermediate care	8.3	26.5
Nursing home days	1.0	11.4
Days at home	44.8	37.9
Surgical procedures	0.51	0.31
Major surgical procedures	0.09	0.01
Minor surgical procedures	0.42	0.30
Radiation treatments‡	7.4	7.7
Chemotherapy treatments	1.3	0.49

*Based on chart review for those patients who died before study conclusion.

‡Over 80% of both hospice and control patients had no radiation treatments. However, those few who did had as many as 48 treatments, hence the large number.

controlled trial of hospice effectiveness in the treatment of terminal cancer patients. We examine several outcomes of hospice care that correspond to the stated goals of the hospice and estimate the costs of hospice and standard care. . . .

Survival Curves

The survival curves for the hospice and control groups were essentially the same. Despite the hospice philosophy of eschewing heroic efforts to extend the life of a dying patient, hospice patients died no sooner than did the controls. One-third of the group died within 45 days after enrollment, the second third within 120 days. The analysis of outcomes was based on data from this period when at least one-third of the subjects were available. The remaining subjects lived for as long as two years. . . .

Hospice patients spent an average of 51 days as inpatients, control patients an average of 47.5 days. There were no statistically significant differences in the total number of days spent in the hospital by hospice and control patients, either in the entire sample or in the sample without out-of-area hospital admission. . . .

Style of Care

Because hospice attempts to improve the patient's last days by reducing or eliminating invasive diagnostic procedures and curtailing treatments such as radiation, chemotherapy, and surgery, one would expect to find fewer of these procedures among hospice patients. Table I reveals only two significant differences between hospice and control groups—major surgical procedures and chemotherapy treatments—for both of which hospice patients had significantly more than controls. The majority of both groups had no treatment. Of hospice patients, 74% had no surgery, 62% no radiation, and 84% no chemotherapy. The corresponding proportions for controls were 82%, 52%, and 84%. The differences in proportions were not statistically significant for any treatment category.

Hospice patients did receive a different style of care. They were treated by a special team in a unit with a heavier staffing ratio than that on the rest of the general hospital wards. This team sought to spend more time with the patient and his family to help them cope more effectively with impending death.

What was the effect of this added effort? At baseline, only 41% of hospice patients and 38% of controls reported pain. Over the course of the study, 34% of hospice and 31% of control subjects *never* reported pain. Neither of these differences was statistically significant. . . .

Significant differences do emerge in satisfaction scores. In two of the three areas examined, hospice patients expressed more satisfaction than did control patients. . . .

No Substantial Difference

Intensive hospice care did not yield the expected benefits in pain or symptom relief or in alleviation of psychological distress when compared with conventional care in a university-affiliated hospital. The differences in satisfaction suggest that both patients and their families appreciated the qualitative differences in hospice care. The pattern of service utilisation suggests that care in this type of hospice is not cheaper than conventional care. Since our findings suggest no substantial difference in cost or effectiveness, we suggest that hospice care should be available as a matter of choice. Some people will want such care; others will opt for more traditional management. . . .

Absence of differences in pain and symptom frequency between hospice and control patients suggests that the hospice may have a lesser role in this technical area than has been suggested. Alternatively, the explanation may be not that hospice care is less effective but that conventional care has become more effective. Better management of pain and symptoms is a medical skill that can be propagated by education. The hospice movement may have made its contribution by sensitising practitioners to their inadequacies.

"*The primary goal of the hospice movement was to change the health care system, not to retreat from it.*"

Hospices Should Remain Outside the Health Care System

Emily K. Abel

Although hospices began as a fringe movement, they became popular in a relatively short period of time and now can be found in many towns and cities. The author of the following viewpoint, Emily K. Abel, argues that this increased popularity has come at a price. Now that hospices are becoming an integral part of the health care system, she believes, the ideals they held have been compromised. Abel works at the Center for the Study of Women at the University of California in Los Angeles.

As you read, consider the following questions:

1. According to Abel, what was the original aim of the hospice movement?
2. Explain the six types of hospices described in the viewpoint.
3. Why does the author object to hospices becoming a part of hospitals?

Emily K. Abel, "The Hospice Movement: Institutionalizing Innovation," *International Journal of Health Services*, Vol. 16, No. 1, 1986. © Baywood Publishing Company. Reprinted with permission.

Since the mid 1970s, hospice programs providing personal and non-technocratic care to the terminally ill have been established throughout the United States. Although they marked a new departure in health care, they bore a striking resemblance to the free schools, food cooperatives, and communes founded several years earlier. If the leaders of the counter-institutions of the 1960s and early 1970s were more likely to adhere to a radical political philosophy than were the major figures of the hospice movement, the two groups shared a number of ideas and attitudes: nostalgia for simple, old fashioned ways, dissatisfaction with bureaucratic and authoritarian institutions, faith in the power of nature, a determination to avoid domination by experts, and a desire to improve the quality of personal relationships. Hospices and the earlier counter-institutions also faced similar problems. Although they originally sought to provide alternatives to the established order, they were forced to rely on mainstream institutions for resources, political acceptance, and personnel. Integration, in turn, compelled them to modify their practices and goals. Based partly on interviews with 15 administrators at hospices in Los Angeles, San Francisco, and New York City, this article argues that, although most hospices began as counter-institutions, they gradually became more traditional. It begins by discussing the similarity of the ideas of the hospice leaders to those of the founders of earlier counter-institutions. It then demonstrates that, as hospices have become better established, they gradually have been incorporated into the dominant health care system and have lost their uniqueness.

Just as free school advocates claimed that the traditional public schools had failed children, so hospice leaders argued that hospitals had proved inadequate to the task of caring for the dying. They overtreated the terminally ill, isolated them from their families, and abandoned them when they were most needy. Early writings from the hospice movement typically opened with a description of a gruesome hospital death, which was then counterposed to the serenity of death in a hospice. But the aim of hospice champions was not simply to comfort a few dying patients. They wanted nothing less than to "revolutionize the American health care system from the inside out." . . .

The Movement Grows

The rapid proliferation of hospices, as of other alternative institutions, often astonished observers. The first hospice in the United States opened its doors in 1974. By 1981, 800 programs were either in existence or being planned. The diversity of forms was equally remarkable. Just as small buying clubs and full-fledged supermarkets were included under the rubric "food cooperatives," so hospices were founded by groups with divergent resources, opportunities, and objectives. One of the major tasks of descriptive studies of hospices has been to classify the varied forms the movement spawned. Paul R. Torrens has defined six separate models:

- self-contained inpatient facilities
- hospital-based free-standing units
- programs located within general hospitals
- symptom-control teams serving patients scattered throughout hospitals
- programs sponsored by home health agencies
- autonomous community-based organizations

But dramatic differences exist even within each category. For example, independent community program budgets range from $1,500 to over $200,000. . . .

Incorporation into the Health Care System

Hospices also could not avoid the influence of institutions they were committed to reforming or replacing. Although the first hospices carefully safeguarded their independence from the established health care system, many edged closer to the mainstream. Some were housed in hospitals or home health agencies; a few were incorporated within nursing homes.

Inherent Problems

There are inherent problems in providing inpatient hospice care in acute-care institutions, because the philosophies underlying the two kinds of care are diametrically opposed. The goal of today's acute-care hospital is sophisticated curative care and maintenance of life; the goal of the hospice is good palliative care and maintenance of dignity.

Elizabeth Gilman McNulty and Robert A. Holderly, *Hospice, A Caring Challenge*, 1983.

Integration had a number of advantages. Institutionally-based hospices tended to avoid duplication of services in their areas. The problems of obtaining licenses or passing Certificate of Need review frequently were eliminated. In some communities, it was not possible to create additional beds, and hospice organizers committed to the inpatient model were forced to obtain the use of excess beds within pre-existing hospitals or nursing homes. Financial benefits were equally compelling. Hospices shared office space, equipment, and often staff with parent institutions. As we will see, though hospices may save money for the health care system as a whole by reducing hospitalization, their services have tended to be more expensive than those of the typical home health agency. Some agencies have been willing to absorb the extra costs, viewing the hospice unit as a "loss leader." Finally, integration satisfied the missionary zeal of hospice leaders. The director of a hospice located within a hospital expressed the hope that "the basic humanism of hospice would radiate to other parts of the hospital."

If affiliation with hospitals or home health agencies helped to spread the values of hospices, however, it also jeopardized their independent identity. When free schools became "educational alternatives" in public school systems, they were compelled to compromise their more radical goals. A study by Robert W. Buckingham and Dale Lupu, showing that hospital-based, in-patient hospices offer fewer psychosocial services than community hospices, suggested that the former tend to adapt to the mold of parent institutions. A few staff members in hospices situated in home health agencies have acknowledged pressures to conform to the regulations and procedures of the sponsoring organizations.

The most serious problems have arisen when hospice programs have not recruited separate staff. Although not all staff members hired directly by hospice administrators have been committed to the hospice mission, they have tended to share a set of ideas and purposes and to cohere as a group. The director of a hospice housed within a nursing home noted that the nurses he inherited were reluctant to follow certain hospice procedures. Although a basic tenet of hospice care is that patients receive pain medication whenever they want, many nurses preferred to adhere to the traditional three-to-four hour schedule to which they were accustomed and which they found more convenient. Moreover, they were horrified by hospice rules permitting dying patients to choose to forego procedures that could prevent malnutrition or dehydration. Although many institutionally-based hospices have avoided such problems by hiring their own staffs, this has not been an option for smaller programs.

The extent of accommodation required also varies with the attitude of the parent organization. The administrators of some hospitals and home health agencies have embraced hospice ideals; others have been reluctant to adapt their regulations to fit the unique characteristics of hospice programs. In the latter case, the result may be, according to one observer, "traditional health care service with hospice overtones." . . .

The Impact of Hospice

In short, hospices have confronted the same problem as other counter-institutions: reliance on the established order for resources, personnel, and acceptance has undermined their ability to offer true alternatives. But we have seen that the primary goal of the hospice movement was to change the health care system, not to retreat from it. Many hospice leaders embraced close association with established medical institutions in order to spread hospice ideals. Indeed, by the early 1980s, directors of hospice programs located within hospitals or home health agencies often pointed with pride to the changes they believed they had wrought in parent organizations. It is impossible to determine the influence of hospices with any certainty: all reformers are prone to exaggerate their effectiveness, and the attitudes of medical staffs toward the hospice philosophy have not been measured. Nevertheless, many hospice leaders were confident that their programs had had a profound impact. One director of a hospice housed in a hospital cited the increased willingness of physicians to refer patients to the hospice unit. Another called attention to the new enthusiasm with which members of the regular medical staff of her institution were learning techniques of pain control from the hospice team. Directors of independent hospice programs were

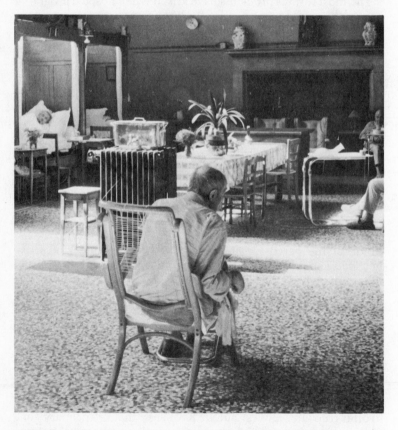

D. Henrioud. Reprinted with permission from the World Health Organization.

equally convinced of their power to influence the medical community. They noted that, though many physicians remained hostile to their movement, others were reorienting their practices to bring them into line with hospice ideas. Approval of the hospice movement by the general public also had increased. It no longer was radical to assert that physicians often lacked sensitivity to the special needs of the dying or that the health care system as a whole placed too much stress on technical feats and too little on compassionate care.

How can we explain the growing appeal of hospices? First, they were part of a larger movement to humanize care for the dying. Hospice founders frequently acknowledged their debt to the pioneering work of Elizabeth Kübler-Ross, who enlarged our understanding of death and dying and campaigned for greater humanity toward the terminally ill. Moreover, hospices incorporated ideas from diverse reform movements within the field of health care. For example, the holistic health movement also demanded that patients be viewed as entire human beings. The women's health movement challenged the sovereignty of physicians and the technological focus of modern medicine; a branch, the home birth movement, criticized the medicalization of pivotal life events. Finally, proponents of self care advocated the demystification of medical knowledge and the promotion of more equitable relationships between patients and physicians.

Conservative Orientation

But, if hospices had roots in progressive reform movements, they also had a conservative orientation. Hospice leaders placed their primary faith in improved relationships between individuals, not in broad structural changes. The concept of the family as the unit of care meshed easily with the conservative campaign to strengthen the family. The central role of volunteers was congenial to groups that viewed charity as the answer to social distress. In short, the increased popularity of the hospice movement can be attributed partly to its ability to appeal simultaneously to both progressives and conservatives.

The growing acceptability of hospice programs tended to blunt the critical force of the movement. . . . Many of the new proponents want to adapt hospice values to institutions that will remain basically unchanged, not to reshape health care in the United States. As the ideas of the hospice movement have been diffused, they also have been diluted and defused. . . .

If the federal government endorses hospices in order to save money, private entrepreneurs create them in order to make money. Many commentators fear that the new benefit will heighten the attractiveness of hospices to private investors. In the past, an infusion of federal funds into new areas in health care has accelerated the shift from nonprofit and governmental organizations to proprietary companies. The danger to the hospice movement may be particularly great because the new Medicare law was passed during a period of rapid private investment in the health care industry. A recent announcement that Donald Getz, the former president of the National Hospice Organization, plans to open a chain of for-profit hospices suggests that the lofty ideals embodied in the movement may not protect it from penetration by private enterprise. Profit-making institutions for the dying will complete the transformation of hospice care from a human service into a commodity. . . .

Deep Social Change Needed

Hospices may have been particularly susceptible to cooptation. Although hospice leaders pointed to the glaring deficiencies of hospital care for the dying and called for a radical reordering of medical priorities, they failed to examine the economic and social forces responsible for the problems they deplored. Believing that social change follows automatically from a change in personal beliefs, they placed their faith in infusing traditional health care institutions with a new set of values. But the technological and curative focus of modern medicine stems not simply from the ideas and attitudes of individual providers but also from financial incentives built into the structure of the health care system. These the hospice movement refrained from addressing.

Medical Consumers

As our Western culture emphasized control over nature, death became the uncontrollable enemy. We gave doctors the responsibility for combatting this enemy. Death became increasingly a medical "problem" instead of a natural event. We gave away the responsibility for death (and life) to experts outside of ourselves—big institutions and big business. . . . People seem to feel that because they invented the machines, they have to use them. So life ends up not to be for living but to justify machinery. We have become medical consumers.

Deborah Duda, *A Guide To Dying at Home*, 1982.

The movement can claim credit for impressive achievements. It enunciated a powerful critique of conventional medical practices and set forth a model of compassionate care. But its history also serves to remind us of the deep and far reaching social changes that will be required before the sick and the dying are treated with dignity.

"[Hospice] care can reach its full potential as it becomes an integral part of our medical care system."

Hospices Should Be Integrated into the Health Care System

Jack M. Zimmerman

In the following viewpoint, Jack M. Zimmerman argues that hospices can be most effective if they become a part of the health care system. By integrating, he believes, hospice workers can teach other doctors and nurses their techniques for relieving the pain and psychological distress of the terminally ill. In addition, hospices would have greater access to the medical technology and specialized care available at a large hospital. Zimmerman is an associate professor at Johns Hopkins University and the Chief of Surgery at Church Hospital in Baltimore. Church Hospital began a hospice program in 1979.

As you read, consider the following questions:

1. Why does the author believe a hospital-based hospice is desirable?
2. Why does Zimmerman consider the idea of hospices which are completely independent of the health care system frightening?

From Jack M. Zimmerman: in HOSPICE: COMPLETE CARE FOR THE TERMINALLY ILL. © 1986, Urban & Schwarzenberg, Baltimore-Munich.

It is difficult to foresee circumstances under which there will not be continuing growth of hospice care programs. An increasing interest and willingness to confront the handling of death and terminal illness, coupled with the results of hospice care programs in action, constitute a compelling argument for the wider use of such programs. Most indications seem to point toward expansion of hospice care. The experience of our program and that of others indicate that there is continuing need for the development of additional hospice programs.

One of the major changes that has occurred in health care delivery generally has been the awakening of concern about cost factors. Whereas a few years ago little attention was directed to control of health care costs, this now has become an important item on the national agenda. A related issue, of course, is the allocation of limited health care resources. Hospice will affect and will be affected by these issues. In precisely what way is open to question.

Diversity of form and style has been one of the strengths of hospice care thus far. Successful hospice programs have adapted to local needs. This should continue. Some free-standing hospices have obviously been enormously productive and have provided valuable knowledge regarding the care of the terminally ill. In some instances they will be the best means of meeting community needs. However, the Church Hospital hospice experience [in Baltimore] and that of other hospital-affiliated programs confirm that the hospital-based hospice is not only a possible but also desirable alternative approach.

The Benefits of Hospital-Based Hospices

There are philosophical, organizational, and financial reasons for promoting the growth of hospital-based units. We hope to see the development and expansion of various types of hospital-based programs. Some will possess a separate facility for hospice patients; some, like Church Hospital's, will have hospice patients integrated with nonhospice patients on a nursing unit; others will have hospice patients distributed throughout the hospital, under treatment by a palliative care team. As new programs are contemplated, those responsible for starting them should examine the options carefully and should design the program best suited to their particular circumstances. Standards for hospice care must be drawn to permit diversity.

As time passes it would perhaps be good if the distinctions between free-standing and hospital-based hospices are blurred. Possibly each hospice program will continue to have a locus at which its administrative function is centered. This may be in a hospital, in a free-standing unit, or in a home care program. However, hospitals, free-standing units, and home care programs serve patients at different levels of care. What is most needed for optimal care of the terminally ill are programs that are truly comprehensive in that they offer continuity of care as the patient shifts from one level to another. In other words, hospice programs should be organized to enable the application of hospice principles and practice across the entire spectrum.

A Modern Hospice's Aims

A modern hospice, whether it is a separate unit or ward, a home care or hospital team, aims to enable a patient to live to the limit of his or her potential in physical strength, mental and emotional capacity, and social relationships. It offers an alternative form of treatment to the acute care of a general hospital, not in opposition but as a further resource for those for whom the usual acute hospital care is no longer appropriate. . . . For the present it appears that a limited number of research and teaching hospices will be needed to establish recognized techniques and standards of care that can be interpreted in the home as well as in other settings. A hospice aim from the start has been that such work should become part of general medical and nursing teaching. . . . Perhaps the team or unit that is part of a hospital complex . . . has the greatest opportunity to integrate with and enrich general practice. The knowledge it contains will form a valuable reference for those working elsewhere in the field.

Cicely Saunders, in *Hospice, Complete Care for the Terminally Ill*, 1986.

It will be imperative for hospital-based programs to offer care not only in the hospital but in the home, as well as to patients who require institutionalization in an intermediate care facility. For many the term nursing home carries very unpleasant connotations. However, there is nothing that makes it categorically impossible for the finest type of hospice care to be available within a nursing home setting. Just as there is nothing that mandates that a hospital providing acute general care cannot offer excellent hospice care, so there is nothing that dictates that a nursing home facility providing care to other patients cannot also render hospice care of the highest caliber. Hospital-based hospice programs should seek to develop suitable arrangements so that they can provide care at the intermediate and home care levels. Often this will require arrangements with existing intermediate care facilities. Decline in hospital occupancy rates as a consequence of cost containment measures may free up some hospital beds for other use. It is not inconceivable, given appropriate financial incentives, that hospitals will opt to develop in-house intermediate care facilities of their own.

Similarly, free-standing hospice units will need to develop formalized arrangements that will permit the preservation of continuity of care when patients require acute hospital care. They will also have to cultivate the types of relationships that permit easy transition between levels of care. They must be certain that patients who would profit from some of the techniques that hospitalization allows are not denied the advantages this would permit.

Comprehensive Care

Programs that begin with a home care base will need to find the means whereby patients can receive care in intermediate facilities and in hospitals without loss of continuity of care.

In other words, whatever the origin and whatever the center of operations, the ultimate aim of hospice programs will have to be the provision of comprehensive care. Otherwise, hospice will run the danger of perpetuating the kind of fragmentation that has plagued the conventional approach it seeks to supplement.

The economics of health care are undoubtedly going to shape the way in which we deal with the terminally ill. Conversely, hospice can have an impact on health care costs. There is an increasing general recognition of the fact that hospice care is an avenue worth exploring in our effort to reduce expenditures for health care without reduction in the quality of that care. There unquestionably will be continued study of this approach, and our experience thus far indicates that hospice care will fare well as a result. However, there is an increasing recognition by many that our financial and other resources for health care are limited and that there must be some thought given to the way in which those resources are allocated, if not rationed. We would be naive if we didn't believe that this poses some threat to the care of the terminally ill. . . .

Hospice Care and Medical Care

Among those of us who have looked carefully at hospice care, one of the principal concerns has been the relationship between hospice care in particular and medical care in general. There are innumerable forms that this relationship could take. At one extreme is the frightening prospect of a totally separate system for the care of the terminally ill, entirely outside of and completely unrelated to the rest of health care. Serious hospice workers would be less than realistic if they considered unthinkable the development of a cultlike phenomenon for the care of the terminally ill. At the opposite extreme is the thought that within the hospice concept are the seeds of a healthy self-destruction, in the course of which hospice care would become completely amalgamated into general medical care, perfusing many of its precepts into the management of acutely ill patients. In truth, it is improbable that the future will take us to either of these extremes. As is often the case, the central part of the spectrum seems to not only more sensible, but also more likely.

Some features of the care of the terminally ill suggest that management of such patients will be, in some respects, a specialty, but one comfortably within the framework of the traditional medical care system. The unique problems faced by the dying are such that they merit the special attention of certain physicians. . . .

If care of the terminally ill is to develop as some form of specialty, hospice care is likely to be part of it. Hospice care possesses some features that make it different from any other medical specialty. One of these is the liberal use of many disciplines and of volunteers. Nonmedical people have played an immense role in the development and conduct of hospice care. They bring to those of us in medicine some perspectives and insights we would not otherwise have. It is to be hoped that they will continue to give of themselves so generously and that the response of physicians and other medical people will be positive. We must watch for and avoid two dangers. Nonmedical people interested in seeing hospice care develop may become so strident that they discourage the participation of medical people and then so frustrated that they decide to move outside the existing health care system. Conversely, medical people may become defensive about what they see as criticism of the way in which they are doing things; they may cease to listen.

Owners of Hospices in the US

	Hospitals		Independent Organizations		Community Agencies		Total	
	N*	%	N	%	N	%	N	%
1982	108	41	103	39	51	19	262	100
1983	174	49	130	37	50	14	354	100

*N = number included in the survey

Reprinted with permission from *The Hospice Project Report*. © the Joint Commission on Accreditation of Hospitals.

Perhaps preservation of the name *hospice* is not the overriding consideration; however, the philosophy and principles that it embodies are. Thus, for those of us interested in the humane care of the terminally ill, our purpose would be achieved if the objectives of hospice were achieved: a clear-cut decision that the patient is incurable, followed by the institution of effective palliation designed to relieve symptoms in the broadest sense for patient and family in the optimal setting, utilizing all of the resources of the multidisciplinary team. . . .

Hospice Principles and Medical Schools

One interesting and anomalous feature of hospice care is that . . . it has developed largely outside our academic institutions, both in England and the United States. This is surprising because seldom in the last several decades has medicine seen something as valuable and with as much potential impact as hospice care develop with so little input from major medical centers and universities. . . .

It is interesting to speculate upon possible reasons for this; understanding them may contribute to correcting what can only be seen as an unfortunate situation. Nonetheless, the only point to be made here is the desirability of university involvement in hospice care in the future. Some might say that if we have gotten this far without them, we do not need them now; they may just complicate things. For several reasons, we do need their interest, support, and involvement. University medical centers are the repositories of resources that hospices need. They possess educational capabilities. It is through the introduction of medical students and house officers to hospice care as a part of the fabric of medical practice that we hope to see the widespread application of hospice principles to the terminally ill. University medical centers have the research capacity, expertise, and experience that can be so valuable to the future care of the terminally ill. This is not to suggest that every university hospital needs to open a hospice unit. There are various means by which academic centers can become involved in hospice care; such involvement would be to the advantage of both the universities and hospices. Put another way, academic institutions and major medical centers possess talents and a stature in our society that can only be ignored at some peril. . . .

Exciting Potential

Experience thus far indicates that the approach embodied in the philosophy and practice of hospice programs offers the potential for better care of the terminally ill at a reasonable cost. Hospice programs are likely to increase in numbers and in quality. Both the art and science of hospice care will grow as experience is gained. Such care can reach its full potential as it becomes an integral part of our medical care system. Dying patients and those who love them deserve no less.

Understanding Words in Context

Readers occasionally come across words which they do not recognize. And frequently, because they do not know a word or words, they will not fully understand the passage being read. Obviously, the reader can look up an unfamiliar word in a dictionary. However, by carefully examining the word in the context in which it is used, the word's meaning can often be determined. A careful reader may find clues to the meaning of the word in surrounding words, ideas, and attitudes.

Below are excerpts from the viewpoints in this chapter. In each excerpt, one or two words are printed in italics. Try to determine the meaning of each word by reading the excerpt. Under each excerpt you will find four definitions for the italicized word. Choose the one that is closest to your understanding of the word.

Finally, use a dictionary to see how well you have understood the words in context. It will be helpful to discuss with others the clues which helped you decide on each word's meaning.

1. Medicine has undergone a profound change in the way it cares for the dying. Spurred by the work of *THANATOLOGISTS,* medical personnel have become more concerned about the quality of patients' last days of life.

   THANATOLOGISTS means:
   a) communists
   b) priests
   c) nurses
   d) people who study death

2. Treatment goals must be set with the patients in mind, not their diseases. For example, chemotherapy which changes the ultimate *PROGNOSIS* very little cannot be justified since it increases fears and discomfort.

   PROGNOSIS means:
   a) funeral
   b) diseased condition
   c) to delay
   d) chances for recovery from illness

3. The doctors and nurses who see death as *PATHOLOGICAL* and not natural often futilely concentrate on curing terminal patients rather than caring for them.

PATHOLOGICAL means:
a) abnormal
b) healthy
c) stupid
d) expensive

4. Blood transfusion rarely improves the quality of life for bedridden patients, but may help an *AMBULATORY* patient function more fully.

AMBULATORY means:
a) friendly
b) walking
c) sleeping
d) energetic

5. It may be good for hospices to self-destruct. They could become completely *AMALGAMATED* into general medical care and teach others their methods.

AMALGAMATED means:
a) confused
b) merged
c) steel company
d) forgotten

6. The explanation may be not that hospice care as an alternative is less effective but that mainstream *CONVENTIONAL* care has become more effective.

CONVENTIONAL means:
a) ordinary
b) drug-related
c) radical
d) non-nuclear weapons

7. The Church Hospital-hospice experience and that of other hospital-*AFFILIATED* programs confirm that the hospital-based hospice works.

AFFILIATED means:
a) likeable
b) rejected
c) associated
d) nursing

Periodical Bibliography

The following list of periodical articles deals with the subject matter of this chapter.

Consumer Reports	"Hospices: Not To Cure But To Help," January 1986.
The Economist	"Hospices: Dying Easier," May 10, 1986.
Michael J. Farrell	"Hospice Approach to Death Still Rare," *National Catholic Reporter,* March 9, 1984.
Ezra M. Greenspan	"Get a Second Opinion on Terminal Care," *The New York Times,* March 26, 1985.
Robert Hirschfield	"Portrait from the Edge," *Christianity & Crisis,* February 17, 1986.
Constance Holden	"Hospices Compared with Conventional Care," *Science,* November 11, 1983.
Peter Jaret	"The Final Guardians," *Newsweek,* December 3, 1984.
Robert L. Kane, Leslie Bernstein, Jeffrey Wales and Rebecca Rothenberg	"Hospice Effectiveness in Controlling Pain," *Journal of the American Medical Association,* May 10, 1985.
Lawrence D. Maloney	"How Hospices Ease Last Days of the Dying," *U.S. News & World Report,* February 11, 1985.
Benita C. Martocchio	"Agendas for Quality of Life," *The Hospice Journal,* Spring 1986.
The Nursing Clinics of North America	"Symposia on Hospice and Compassionate Care and the Dying Experience," June 1985.
Allan Parachini	"Hospices Rated Only on Par with Hospitals," *Los Angeles Times,* May 1, 1984.
Robert Rodale	"Caring and Sharing," *Prevention,* March 1983.
Cicely Saunders	"Care of the Dying," *World Health,* November 1982.
Philip R. Sullivan	"Hospice or Hospital?" *America,* February 2, 1985.
Claire Tehan	"Has Success Spoiled Hospice?" *Hastings Center Report,* October 1985.

Organizations To Contact

American Association of Suicidology
2459 S. Ash
Denver, CO 80222
(303) 692-0985

Founded in 1967, the Association includes people from various disciplines and fields who share a common interest in advancing the study of suicide prevention and life-threatening behavior. It publishes the quarterlies *Newslink* and *Suicide and Life-Threatening Behavior.*

American Civil Liberties Union (ACLU)
22 E. 40th St.
New York, NY 10016
(212) 944-9800

The ACLU was founded in 1920. It champions the rights of individuals in right-to-die and euthanasia cases as well as in many other civil rights issues. The Foundation of the ACLU provides legal defense, research, and education. The organization publishes the quarterly *Civil Liberties* and various pamphlets, books, and position papers.

American Coalition of Citizens with Disabilities (ACCD)
1012 14th St. NW, Suite 901
Washington, DC 20005
(202) 628-3470

The Coalition's goal is to safeguard and promote full human and constitutional rights for the disabled. It opposes infant euthanasia decisions which discriminate against handicapped babies. ACCD publishes books and a quarterly newsletter, *ACCD NewsNet.*

American Medical Association (AMA)
535 N. Dearborn St.
Chicago, IL 60610
(312) 645-5000

Among the AMA's many purposes, it informs its members of new scientific information and new legislation affecting medicine. The AMA's committees on medical ethics have suggested guidelines for euthanasia and hospital policy. Two of its weekly publications are the *Journal of the American Medical Association* and *American Medical News.*

Americans United for Life (AUL)
343 S. Dearborn St.
Chicago, IL 60604
(312) 786-9494

AUL has expanded its activities to all areas where the sacredness of human life is challenged—fetuses, handicapped newborns, the elderly, and comatose patients. It publishes a newsletter every six weeks as well as the quarterly *Youth Crusaders News.*

Center for Death Education and Research
1167 Social Science Building
University of Minnesota
267 19th Ave. S
Minneapolis, MN 55455
(612) 624-1895

This pioneering program in death education, founded in 1969, sponsors original research into grief and bereavement as well as studies of attitudes and responses to death and dying. The Center conducts television, newspaper, and university classes and workshops for the care-giving professions. A list of published materials is available upon request.

Concern for Dying
250 W. 57th St.
New York, NY 10107
(212) 246-6962

This organization was founded in 1967 with the purpose of informing and educating the general public and medical, legal, and health care professionals on the problems and needs of terminally ill patients and their families. Its goal is to assure patient autonomy with regard to treatment, and the prevention of futile prolongation of the dying process. It publishes *A Legal Guide to the Living Will, Euthanasia: A Decade of Change,* and the quarterly *Concern for Dying Newsletter.*

Disability Rights Education and Defense Fund
2212 6th St.
Berkeley, CA 94710
(415) 644-2555

This organization works to further the civil rights and liberties of the disabled. It maintains a Disability Law National Support Center which identifies key disability issues. In the past, it has opposed infant euthanasia decisions which discriminate against the handicapped. It publishes the quarterly *Disability Rights Review* and handbooks.

Forum for Death Education and Counseling
2211 Arthur Ave.
Lakewood, OH 44107
(216) 228-0334

The Forum works to improve death education and counseling in hospitals and among health care workers. It prepares educational materials, holds workshops, and publishes a newsletter.

Foundation of Thanatology
630 W. 168th St.
New York, NY 10032
(212) 694-4173

This organization of health, theology, psychology, and social science professionals is devoted to scientific and humanist inquiries into death, loss, grief, and bereavement. The Foundation, formed in 1967, coordinates professional, educational, and research programs concerned with mortality and grief. It publishes annual directories and the periodicals *Advances in Thanatology* and *Archives of the Foundation of Thanatology.*

The Hastings Center
360 Broadway

Hastings-on-Hudson, NY 10706
(914) 478-0500

Since its founding in 1969, The Hastings Center has played a central role in raising issues as a response to advances in medicine, the biological sciences, and the social and behavioral sciences. In examining the wide range of moral, social, and legal questions, the Center has established three goals: advancement of research on the issues, stimulation of universities and professional schools to support the teaching of ethics, and public education. It publishes *The Hastings Center Report*.

Hemlock Society
PO Box 66218
Los Angeles, CA 90066
(213) 391-1871

Founded in 1980, the Society supports active voluntary euthanasia for the terminally ill. It does not encourage suicide for anyone who is not terminally ill; it approves suicide prevention programs. The Society believes that the final decision to terminate one's life is one's own. It publishes a *Right To Die* newsletter and several books on euthanasia and suicide.

Hospice Education Institute (HEI)
PO Box 713
5 Essex Square, Suite 3-B
Essex, CT 06426
(203) 767-1620

HEI was founded in 1985. It provides information to the public and medical care professionals on hospice care and bereavement counseling.

Human Life Center (HLC)
St. John's University
Collegeville, MN 56321
(612) 363-3313

HLC is sponsored by St. John's University, a Catholic university for men. It promotes the sanctity of life ethic and publishes the periodical *Human Life Issues* in addition to pamphlets opposing euthanasia and infant euthanasia.

Human Life International
418 C St. NE
Washington, DC 20002
(202) 546-2257

This pro-life organization serves as a research, educational, and service program. Its topics include Christian sexuality, infanticide, and euthanasia. It publishes *Death Without Dignity* and *Deceiving Birth Controllers*.

Joint Commission on Accreditation of Hospitals (JCAH)
875 N. Michigan Ave.
Chicago, IL 60611
(312) 642-6061

The JCAH sets standards for hospitals, hospices, and other medical facilities. It has conducted studies on hospices and publishes *Quality Review Bulletin* and *Perspectives*.

National Committee on Youth Suicide Prevention
666 5th Ave., 13th Floor
New York, NY 10103
(212) 957-9292

The Committee is a network of volunteers. It encourages youth suicide prevention programs in schools and communities and publishes brochures on suicide.

National Hospice Organization
1901 N. Fort Meyer Dr., Suite 402
Arlington, VA 22209
(703) 243-5900

The organization promotes the hospice, "a concept of caring for the terminally ill and their families which enables the patient to live as fully as possible, makes the entire family the unit of care, and centers the caring process in the home when appropriate." It conducts educational and training programs in hospice care for administrators and caregivers and publishes pamphlets.

National Right to Life Committee, Inc.
419 7th St. NW, Suite 402
Washington, DC 20004
(202) 638-4396

The Committee, founded in 1973, opposes abortion and euthanasia. It provides ongoing public education programs on abortion, euthanasia, and infanticide and maintains a printed library with over 430 volumes. It publishes *National Right to Life News*, a bimonthly periodical, and a pamphlet entitled *Challenge to Be Pro-Life*.

National Save-A-Life League
815 2nd Ave., Suite 409
New York, NY 10017
(212) 492-4668

This organization of professionals and trained volunteers was founded in 1906 to work toward the prevention of suicide and to counsel families of suicide victims. The organization maintains a crisis center, provides a speakers bureau, sponsors educational radio programs on suicide, and offers financial aid and referrals. It maintains a 24-hour hotline.

Parents of Suicides (PS)
321 Prospect Ave.
Hackensack, NJ 07601
(201) 343-3908

PS is a support group for bereaved parents and siblings of people who have committed suicide. It has a small library, provides speakers to schools and the media, and publishes a monthly newsletter.

St. Francis Center
1768 Church St. NW
Washington, DC 20036
(202) 234-5613

The Center provides a broad range of services to individuals, families, and professionals dealing with life-threatening illness, bereavement, and loss. Founded in 1973, the non-denominational Center has expanded its services from alternatives to commercial funeral practices to counseling, education, and support programs.

Samaritans
500 Commonwealth Ave.
Kenmore Square
Boston, MA 02215
(617) 247-0220

The Samaritans are volunteers who try to prevent suicide by befriending depressed and suicidal people. They offer walk-in counseling and 24-hour emergency service for suicidal people.

Shanti Nilaya
PO Box 2396
Escondido, CA 92025
(714) 749-2008

Shanti Nilaya was founded by Elisabeth Kübler-Ross. It holds regular retreats and workshops for dying patients, their families, and professionals.

Society for the Right To Die
250 W. 57th St.
New York, NY 10107
(212) 246-6973

The Society advances nationwide recognition and protection of an individual's right to die with dignity. It distributes "living will" forms and publishes legislative and judicial information. The organization serves as a clearinghouse for health professionals, educators, attorneys, lawmakers, the media, and the general public. It aids citizen committees to further patients' rights and conducts awareness campaigns to disseminate rights information.

Suicide Prevention and Crisis Center
1811 Trousdale Dr.
Burlingame, CA 94010
(415) 877-5604

Founded in 1965, the center disseminates information about suicide prevention, arranges specialized training of persons in suicide prevention, and carries out research programs. It publishes a quarterly newsletter.

TASH: The Association for Persons with Severe Handicaps
7010 Roosevelt Way NE
Seattle, WA 98115
(206) 523-8446

TASH is a national organization of parents, administrators, teachers, medical personnel, researchers, and other interested people dedicated to making appropriate education and services available for severely handicapped people from birth to adulthood.

The Value of Life Committee, Inc.
637 Cambridge St.
Brighton, MA 02135
(617) 787-4400

The Committee, founded in 1970, is concerned with fostering respect for human life from fertilization to natural death. In addition, they strive to inform the general public regarding issues concerning life such as ethics, euthanasia, and genetics. The Committee disseminates dozens of articles and papers in support of its position.

Youth Suicide National Center (YSNC)
1825 Eye St. NW, Suite 400
Washington, DC 20006
(202) 429-2016

The Center's work focuses on developing education and prevention programs on teen suicide. YSNC, founded in 1985, coordinates youth suicide education programs. Its president is Charlotte P. Ross, a leading proponent of suicide education programs.

Bibliography of Books

Lewis R. Aiken — *Dying, Death, and Bereavement.* Boston: Allyn and Bacon, 1985.

A. Alvarez — *The Savage God: A Study of Suicide.* New York: Random House, 1972.

Margaret Pabst Battin and David J. Mayo, eds. — *Suicide: The Philosophical Issues.* New York: St. Martin's Press, 1980.

Jayne Blankenship — *In the Center of the Night: Journey Through a Bereavement.* New York: G.P. Putnam's Sons, 1984.

Robert W. Buckingham — *The Complete Hospice Guide.* New York: Harper & Row, 1983.

Amnon Carmi — *Euthanasia.* New York: Springer-Verlag, 1984.

David Carroll — *Living with Dying.* New York: McGraw Hill Book Company, 1985.

B.D. Colen — *Born at Risk.* New York: St. Martin's Press, 1981.

B.D. Colen — *Hard Choices: Mixed Blessings of Modern Medical Technology.* New York: G.P. Putnam's Sons, 1986.

Patricia A. Davis — *Suicidal Adolescents.* Springfield, IL: Charles C. Thomas Publisher, 1983.

Melinda Delahoyde — *Fighting for Life: Defending the Newborn's Right To Live.* Ann Arbor, MI: Servant Books, 1984.

Melinda Delahoyde and Dennis J. Horan, eds. — *Infanticide and the Handicapped Newborn.* Provo, UT: Brigham Young University Press, 1982.

Lynne Ann DeSpelder and Albert Lee Strickland — *The Last Dance: Encountering Death and Dying.* Palo Alto, CA: Mayfield Publishing Company, 1983.

Edward F. Dobihal and Charles William Stewart — *When a Friend Is Dying.* Nashville, IN: Abingdon Press, 1984.

Karen Gardner, ed. — *Quality of Care for the Terminally Ill.* Chicago: Joint Commission on Accreditation of Hospitals, 1985.

Rasa Gustaitis and Ernlé Young — *A Time To Be Born, A Time To Die: Conflicts and Ethics in an Intensive Care Nursery.* Reading, MA: Addison Wesley, 1986.

Keith Hawton — *Suicide and Attempted Suicide Among Children and Adolescents.* Beverly Hills, CA: Sage Publications, 1986.

Derek Humphrey — *Let Me Die Before I Wake.* New York: Grove Press, 1984.

Derek Humphrey and Ann Wickett — *The Right To Die.* New York: Harper & Row, 1986.

Donald W. Knowles and Nancy Reeves — *But Won't Granny Need Her Socks?* Dubuque, IA: Kendall/Hunt Publishing Company, 1983.

C. Everett Koop	*The Right To Live, The Right To Die.* Toronto: Life Cycle Books, 1980.
Elisabeth Kübler-Ross	*Living with Death and Dying.* New York: Macmillan Publishing Company, 1981.
Elisabeth Kübler-Ross	*Working It Through.* New York: Macmillan Publishing Company, 1982.
Austin H. Kutscher, Samuel C. Klagsbrun, et al.	*Hospice U.S.A.* New York: Columbia University Press, 1983.
Christopher Leach	*Letter to a Younger Son.* New York: Harcourt Brace Jovanovich, 1981.
Deborah Whiting Little	*Home Care for the Dying.* Garden City, NY: The Dial Press/Doubleday, 1985.
Jeff Lyon	*Playing God in the Nursery.* New York: W.W. Norton & Company, 1985.
James Manney and John C. Blattner	*Death in the Nursery: The Secret Crime of Infanticide.* Ann Arbor, MI: Servant Books, 1984.
Ernest Morgan	*Dealing Creatively with Death.* Burnsville, NC: Celo Press, 1984.
Anne Munley	*The Hospice Alternative.* New York: Basic Books, 1983.
Nancy O'Connor	*Letting Go with Love: The Grieving Process.* Apache Junction, AZ: La Mariposa Press, 1984.
Elizabeth Ogg	*Facing Death and Loss.* Lancaster, PA: Technomic Publishing Company, 1985.
Michael L. Peck, Norman L. Farberow, and Robert E. Litman	*Youth Suicide.* New York: Springer Publishing Company, 1985.
Robert A. Raab	*Coping with Death.* New York: The Rosen Publishing Group, 1983.
James Rachels	*The End of Life.* New York: Oxford University Press, 1986.
William V. Rauscher	*The Case Against Suicide.* New York: St. Martin's Press, 1981.
Charles E. Rice	*Beyond Abortion: The Theory and Practice of the Secular State.* Chicago: Franciscan Herald Press, 1979.
Betty Rollin	*Last Wish.* New York: Simon & Schuster, 1985.
Jo Roman	*Exit House: Choosing Suicide as an Alternative.* New York: Seaview Books, 1980.
Jay F. Rosenberg	*Thinking Clearly About Death.* Englewood Cliffs, NJ: Prentice-Hall, 1983.
Cicely Saunders, Dorothy H. Summers, and Neville Teller, eds.	*Hospice: The Living Idea.* Philadelphia: W.B. Saunders Company, 1981.

Sylvia H. Schraff   *Hospice: The Nursing Perspective.* New York: National League for Nursing, 1984.

Earl E. Shelp   *Born To Die? Deciding the Fate of Critically Ill Newborns.* New York: The Free Press, 1986.

Paul D. Simmons   *Birth and Death: Biomedical Decision-Making.* Philadelphia: Westminster Press, 1983.

Averil Stedeford   *Facing Death.* London: William Heinemann Medical Books, 1984.

Bonnie Steinbock, ed.   *Killing and Letting Die.* Englewood Cliffs, NJ: Prentice-Hall, 1980.

Robert and Peggy Stinson   *The Long Dying of Baby Andrew.* Boston: Little, Brown and Company, 1983.

Margot Tallmer, Elizabeth R. Prichard, et al.   *The Life-Threatened Elderly.* New York: Columbia University Press, 1984.

Michael Tooley   *Abortion and Infanticide.* New York: Oxford University Press, 1983.

Paul B. Torrens, ed.   *Hospice Programs and Public Policy.* Chicago: American Hospital Publishing, 1985.

Paul Tsongas   *Heading Home.* New York: Knopf, 1984.

Samuel E. Wallace and Albin Eser   *Suicide and Euthanasia: The Rights of Personhood.* Knoxville, TN: University of Tennessee Press, 1981.

Jeffrey A. Watson   *Looking Beyond: A Christian View of Suffering and Death.* Wheaton, IL: Victor Books, 1986.

Susan White-Bowden   *Everything To Live For.* New York: Poseidon Press, 1985.

William J. Winslade and Judith Wilson Ross   *Choosing Life or Death: A Guide for Patients, Families and Professionals.* New York: The Free Press, 1986.

Jack M. Zimmerman   *Hospice: Complete Care for the Terminally Ill,* 2d edition. Baltimore, MD: Urban & Schwarzenberg, 1986.

Index

and friends' help, 38-42
and psychotherapy, 21, 22, 26-27
and support groups, 43-47
can be private, 34-36
counseling of, 28-33
delayed, 19-21
distorted, 21-22
emotions of, 17, 19, 21, 28
follows a pattern, 16-22
as inaccurate, 23-27
in other societies, 25, 35-36
in Western culture, 26, 35-36
necessity of, 17
phases of, 18-19, 35
should be shared, 28-33
ways to help, 39-42

handicapped infants
cases
Baby Doe, 98, 120
Baby Jane Doe, 107-110, 120-123
Bailey baby, 104-106
Oklahoma experiments, 112, 113, 116
Stinson baby, 94, 105, 129
treatment of
and neonatal intensive care units, 127, 130
as doctors' decision, 124-130
as parents' decision, 100, 103-110, 120, 126
needs government involvement, 114-117
con, 124-130
Heilig, Sam M., 58
Henrioud, D., 192
Hentoff, Nat, 112, 118
Heyderbrand, Wolf, 175
Hilger, Andy, 79
Holderly, Robert A., 177, 190
home care, 180
hospices
and medical insurance, 177
as an aid to grief, 183
as no longer unique, 188-194
as unique, 199
compared to hospitals, 173-178, 184-187
costs of, 190, 198
description of, 176, 180, 189, 190, 196
goals of, 176, 180-182, 197, 198
history of, 176, 189, 192
provide best care for the dying, 179-183
within hospitals, 177-178, 179-183, 195-200
hospitals

and treatment of the dying, 173-178, 181
are as effective as hospices, 184-187
as bureaucracies, 174-175
as impersonal, 174-175
Hurwitz, Howard, 69

infant euthanasia, 89-130
and abortion, 94-95, 98-99
and "Baby Doe" rule, 122, 123, 125, 126
and the "child's best interests," 114, 115
and definition of human life, 90-96, 116, 126
and disability rights groups, 121-122
and handicapped infants, 98-102
and neonatal intensive care units, 127, 130
and quality of life, 89-96, 98-99, 103-110, 113, 116, 127, 129
and "right to life," 91, 96, 102
and sanctity of life, 90, 93-94
and "slippery slope," 95, 98-100, 116
as discrimination, 118-123
as doctors' decision, 125-130
con, 99-102, 105, 110, 113-117, 118-123
as murder, 98, 112
as parents' decision, 100, 103-110, 126
con, 98, 113-117
cases
Baby Doe, 98, 120
Baby Jane Doe, 107-110, 120-123
Bailey baby, 104-106
Oklahoma experiment, 112, 113, 116
Stinson baby, 94, 105, 129
ethics of, 94-96, 97-102, 113-115
history of, 96, 106, 117
is never justified, 97-102
may be justified, 89-96
need for government involvement, 114-117, 118-123
con, 124-130
infanticide, see infant euthanasia
Institute of Medicine, 25, 26
International Association for Suicide Prevention, 54

Jackson, Edgar N., 18
Jasper, William F., 71
Javits, Jacob K., 150
Jefferson, Thomas, 47
Joyce, Christopher, 23

213